SPALDING®

Defensive Baseball

Rod Delmonico, M.Ed.
Head Baseball Coach, University of Tennessee

MP
MASTERS PRESS

A Division of Howard W. Sams & Company
A Bell Atlantic Company

Masters Press (A Division of Howard W. Sams & Co.)
2647 Waterfront Parkway, East Drive, Suite 300
Indianapolis, IN 46214

Library of Congress Cataloging-in-Publication Data

Defensive Baseball /
Rod Delmonico
    p. cm.
    ISBN: 1-57028-029-0: $14.95
    1. Baseball--Defense.
    2. Fielding (Baseball)
    I. Title.

GV867.7.D45 1995
796.357'24 – dc20

95-45580
CIP

Foreword

Home runs may bring baseball fans to their feet, but more often than not, it's defense rather than hitting that determines the outcome of a game.

A popular philosophy among the baseball coaching fraternity is that good defense and good pitching can overcome good hitting. It is a philosophy backed by statistics. That's why this book is important. It not only stresses the importance of playing good defense but it goes the extra mile with pictures, diagrams and explanations to teach coaches and players how to be a good defensive team.

At LSU, we have had the good fortune of winning two national championships. We couldn't have done that without a solid defensive effort from our fielders and pitchers. As members of the Southeastern Conference, we play Rod Delmonico's teams on a regular basis, and we know whenever we play Tennessee we will face a team that is prepared both mentally and physically to play defense.

There is no doubt that hitting is important to the success of every team. But a team that is prepared and able to execute the defensive plays in the field will undoubtedly win more games than it loses.

Skip Bertman, head coach, Louisiana State University
1991 and 1993 National Champions
Head coach, 1996 U.S. Olympic Team

I want to thank all my coaching friends over the years that have helped me along the way. A special thanks to Bill Wilhelm, Mike Martin and Skip Bertman. A special thanks to Janie Cormack for countless hours of typing the manuscript.

This book is affectionately dedicated to my wife, Barb and my three sons, Tony, Joey and Nicky for allowing me to take time apart from them to author this book.

Table of Contents

1 — Pitching **1**

Basic Delivery (no one on base) 1

Pitching from the Stretch 5

Stopping the Running Game 6

Holding Runners at First 6

Timing the Pitcher's Move 7

Idiosyncrasies 8

Runner on Second 8

Runner on Third 9

Pickoff Move 10

Grips and Deliveries 11

Fielding 15

2 — Catcher **17**

Giving Signs 18

Receiving 19

Catching the Outside Pitch 21

Catching the Low Pitch 22

Blocking Pitches 23

Fielding Bunts 26

Strike Three, Ball in the Dirt 28

Throwing 29

Catching Pop-ups 31

Tag Plays 32

3 — Infield Play **33**

Ready Position 33

Reading Pitches to Get a Jump on the Ball 35

Catching a Ball Hit Directly at the Fielder 36

Catching the Ball 37

Short Hops 39

Throwing 40

Lateral Movement 40

Forehand Play 41
Backhand Play 43
45-Degree Angles 44
Receiving Throws at First Base 45

4 — First Base 45

Balls in the Dirt 48
Holding Runners 50
Throwing to Second Base 51
Fielding Bunts and Slow Rollers 52
Throws to the Pitcher Covering First 52
Bunt Plays 53

5 — Shortstop and Second Base 55

Feeds from the Shortstop 56
Ball Hit Directly at the Shortstop 56
Ball Hit to his Backhand 57
Ball Hit to his Left 57
Slow-Hit Ground Ball 58
Shortstop Pivots 58
Inside Pivot 59
Shortstop Unassisted 59
Second Base Pivots 60
Feeds from the Second Baseman 65
Ground Ball Hit Directly at the Second Baseman 65
Ground Ball Hit to the Second Baseman's Right 66
A Slowly Hit Ball in the Baseline 66
Balls Hit to the Extreme Left 67
Tag Plays 68

6 — Third Base 69

Slow Roller.. 70
Backhand Play 72
Bunting Situations 74
Double Play Balls 75

7 — Outfield Play 77

Ball Hit Directly at the Outfielder 77
Rounding a Fly Ball 79
Fly Ball Hit Over Outfielder's Head 79
Reverse Pivots 80
Catching The "Do-or-Die" Ground Ball 81
Ball Hit to the Left or Right 82
Playing the Fence 83
Play in the Sun 86
Dive Plays 86
Communication 87
Backing Up Bases 88

8 — Team Defense 89

Defensive Alignment 89
Bunt Defense 96
Rundowns 101
Passed Ball and Wild Pitch Defense 103
Relays 104
Cutoffs 106
Pop Fly Communications 107
First and Third Defense 109

Situations: Relays and Cutoffs 111

Credits:

Cover design by Kelli Ternet
Edited by Kim Heusel
Photographic reproduction assistance by Terry Varvel
Text layout by Kim Heusel
Proofread by Pat Brady
Cover photo by Nick Myers
Interior photos by Chip Baker, Lisa Clanton, Pepper Martin and Nick Myers

Defensive Baseball

1
Pitching

Good hitting and good baserunning can win baseball games. But good defense can take it a step farther: It can win championships.

Good defense starts right up there on the pitching mound. Give a coach a pitching staff that can throw strikes, hit locations and keep the offense off balance, and he'll let you have the bats.

All the heavy thinkers agree: ***Good pitching gets out good hitting,*** and they will spend hours every day teaching every pitcher the mechanics of a smooth, economic delivery, pitching from the stretch position, pickoff moves, fielding the position and working on the hitters.

Every pitching delivery must originate from a balanced and relaxed stance that will enable the pitcher to deliver the ball smoothly, easily and with maximum efficiency — meaning without any wasted motion. The pitcher must develop a simple, uncomplicated delivery. The simpler it is, the greater the chances of throwing strikes consistently.

Basic Delivery (no one on base)

Years ago, practically every pitcher started his motion with an arm pump and windup that brought the ball overhead before the leg kick.

The pump and windup were intended to establish a rhythm and a momentum, and they did. But this extra motion was biomechanically suspect. It created extra movement and increased the risk of error. It became harder to throw strikes and more energy was consumed on every pitch.

For all these reasons, many coaches started reconsidering the pump and windup. They wanted the pitchers to throw with a simple, uncomplicated delivery that would put less strain on the arm and make for greater control and efficiency.

Check Sequence 1-1. This is the kind of delivery we teach at Tennessee. We want the pitcher to assume an upright but relaxed position facing the plate with both feet on the rubber.

1

Sequence 1-1

If the pitcher is right-handed, we want him to set up on the right side of the rubber. If he is left-handed, we want him to set up on the left side enabling him to deliver the ball from an angle rather than straight on.

Let's assume the pitcher is right-handed. (Reverse all the following directions if he is left-handed.) That means his right foot will be the pivot foot. We want him to place the front spike in front of the rubber and the back spike on the front edge or top of the rubber.

The left (stride) foot should be set so that the back spike is behind the rubber and the front spike on or just touching the rubber. In short, the feet are set fairly close together, in a heel-toe relationship, with the weight resting on the stride (left) foot.

> ***Coaching Point:*** *If, as the game goes along, the pitcher runs into control problems, he can adjust his position on the rubber to the right or left, depending upon the problem.*

As shown in Sequence 1-2, we want the pitcher to face the hitter squarely with his head up and his shoulders in a slightly concave position which should make him feel more relaxed.

Sequence 1-2

Note how the ball is held in the glove with the back of the glove facing out to conceal the ball. The right (pitching) hand is held loosely down the other side.

After getting the sign from the catcher, the pitcher should bring his hands together at about chest height, with the glove just out in front, covering the ball and hand while reaching in to get his grip.

In this set position, the glove is held as if the pitcher were reading a book, with the back of the "book" concealing the "words" (ball) from prying eyes.

This is why we want our pitchers to use large gloves. Such gloves help them conceal the pitching grip from the batter and third-base coach as well as help him field the ball and easily handle all the catcher's throws.

The pitcher will start his delivery with a rocker action. He'll take a small jab step (about 8 to 12 inches) straight back with the left (stride) foot, and then slide his right (pivot) foot into a parallel position alongside of the rubber.

This foot becomes the fulcrum for the delivery.

The pitcher must now pivot on this foot and rotate his body to the other side. As shown in Photo 1-1, he raises his front (stride) leg at least parallel to the ground, which puts him into the gather position from which he will unleash his drive to the plate.

3

The body is balanced over the back foot, with the knee parallel (or slightly higher) to the ground, and the back knee flexed. The hands stay up in front, with the ball buried in the glove where no one can read the grip.

Coaching Point: *If the gather position is effected correctly, the pitcher will be able to hold it for several seconds without falling left or right. The better the balance, the better the mechanics and the better the end result — good pitches.*

Photo 1-1

Remember, the front leg is not kicked out or up as this can throw the motion off balance. The leg is lowered and driven straight for the plate, with the hips applying the driving force and the bent pivot foot applying the extra push off the ground.

The extension of the left arm (forward) and the right arm (backward) brings the pitcher to what we call the T position. (Photo 1-2)

From this point, the pitcher will step straight for the plate, with the hips supplying the driving force and the bent pivot foot furnishing an extra push off the ground.

We tell our pitchers to "ride your legs to the plate" to get the most out of their lower body. We don't want to waste any time on dropping and driving which is like throwing "uphill" at the plate. We want them to simply drive to the plate — "ride" their legs.

The pitcher should take a comfortably long stride and land on the ball of his foot with his knee slightly bent and his foot slightly closed at a 45-degree angle. The foot should land on the same spot every time from 3 to 6 inches inside an imaginary line running from the pivot foot to the plate.

The arm should follow through naturally over to the opposite side and the back foot should be brought forward to a parallel position with the stride foot, squaring off the pitcher with the plate. This puts him in perfect position to field anything hit to either side or right back at him.

A note about the follow-through: It doesn't really add or subtract from the pitch. Once the ball leaves the hand, that's it. The pitcher can't do anything more with it.

Photo 1-2

What the follow-through does do is indicate the quality of the pitch — whether the ball has been properly delivered. If the pitcher is not landing in the correct spot or falling off to the right or left, the chances are that he is doing something wrong.

Key: Whenever a pitcher has to throw 100 to 140 pitches a game, you don't want him to waste energy on needless motion — the less body movement, the better. Such pointless movements as bending over at the waist in taking signs or lifting the hands above the head (winding up) waste energy and zap strength.

Key: Coaches should check every motion of the pitcher to determine whether it is extraneous or whether it is exposing the pitching grip. In this day of the super spy, managers and coaches have become experts at spotting giveaways in a pitcher's delivery.

Pitching from the Stretch

After learning the basic delivery from the set position, the pitcher should have no problem learning how to pitch from the stretch, which really isn't a stretch but a mild variation of the no-windup regular delivery.

Again we try to eliminate as much excess body movement as possible. Instead of letting the pitcher take the sign by bending over at the waist, with his hands on the knees, we have him stand upright with slightly concave shoulders, his feet shoulder-width apart and his gloved hand (with the ball in it) down by his side.

He goes to the set position by taking a jab step forward with the left foot (for right-handed pitchers) and bringing his hands up to his chest. As shown in Sequence 1-3, he grips the ball in his gloved hand with the elbows pointing down.

Sequence 1-3

In this position, he can glance over his left shoulder to check the runner's lead at first. This simple, uncomplicated stance, so closely resembling the basic pitching stance, will enable the pitcher to throw to any base without any elaborate variation in pitching motion.

He must, of course, minimize his kicking action to avoid giving the runners a jump. Here you can see in Sequence 1-4 how the pitcher simply kicks and rides his leg to the plate.

Sequence 1-4

Stopping the Running Game

Teams with a lot of speed can literally run a poor defensive club out of the park. True, nobody can steal first base, but once your speedster gets there, he can run an unprepared defense dizzy. The best way to stop the running game, of course, is by not allowing anyone to reach first. Since that's not likely to happen, start by getting your pitcher to throw strikes and keeping walks to a minimum.

At the same time, you don't want your pitcher to throw a lot of fat pitches or to start throwing all fastballs. You'll soon find the hitters sitting back and waiting on the fastball.

Smart pitchers will make the runner (and hitter) think fastball and then come in with off-speed and breaking pitches. In short, they will try to get the hitter out with their best pitches.

Holding Runners at First

Once the good base runner gets to first, his job will be to set the tone for the running game. He'll be aggressive, always trying to make something happen via a steal or a wild throw to first.

The pitcher's job is to hold the runner at first — hinder his timing, break his concentration, keep him off stride, see that he doesn't dig in and get that big jump. He must make the runner uncomfortable and discourage him from being aggressive.

Many runners will try to:

1) Run early in the count.

2) Look for an off-speed pitch.

3) Attempt to read some idiosyncrasy of the pitcher.

The runner who likes to go early in the count will usually be looking for a breaking ball on the first or second pitch. The pitcher can defeat him by either pitching out or throwing a fastball.

This kind of pitching strategy will tend to slow down the offensive-minded manager. It will put the thought of pitchout in his mind, making him timid about putting on the steal sign.

Pitchers who show the runner different looks or who vary their kicks to the plate will throw off the base stealer's timing.

It's important for every pitcher to change his rhythm once in a while. He doesn't want to always come to the set position and throw to first or home. I want my pitchers to mix their approach. First, to kick and throw to the plate. Next, to hold for three or four seconds, then kick and throw.

The variety in rhythm will impair the runner's timing and make it difficult for him to get a great jump. Breaking the runner's concentration and making him think pickoff gives your pitcher an edge.

Unbelievably, some pitchers never throw to first base more than once or twice. Once the runner becomes aware of this, he'll start licking his chops. After the pitcher throws over for the second time, the runner will get that great jump on the next pitch.

Pitchers have to be taught to mix 'em up — sometimes throw to first three or four times in a row, using variations in set, hold and throw. Remember, you have to teach your pitchers how to do this without tinkering with their mechanics.

Timing the Pitcher's Move

The average college pitcher will deliver the ball somewhere between 1.3 and 1.6 seconds (fastball) from kick to catcher's mitt. He will take a little longer on his curve or change-up — somewhere between 1.5 and 1.9.

The good college catcher will take somewhere from 1.9 to 2.1 seconds to get the ball down to second after it hits his mitt.

If you combine these times (fastball 3.2 to 3.7 and curveball 3.4 to 4.0) and remember that the average runner with a 10-foot lead can go from first to second in 3.5 seconds, you can see what kind of problems this will pose for your defense.

Since the average pitcher-catcher combination will usually lean toward the higher end of the spectrum, it is sometimes impossible to nail even the average runner. Today's fastest base runners can make it to second in about 3.3 seconds. What can you do about this?

1) By simply speeding up the pitcher's delivery, getting him to deliver in about 1.1 to 1.2, you'll help give your catcher a better chance.

2) Have the pitcher cut his leg kick down. Teach him to use a simple slide step to the plate. This modified leg kick will reduce his delivery time and give the battery a better combined delivery time — about 3.1 to 3.3 seconds, thus making it almost impossible for the average runner to steal.

Idiosyncrasies

Every pitcher — left-handed or right-handed — exhibits some idiosyncrasy every time he throws to the plate or first base. Some quirks are more obvious than others, and it is essential for coaches and teammates to check their pitchers for any kind of give-away that will give the runners an advantage.

For example, your typical left-handed pitcher will look home and throw to first, or look at first and throw home. All the runner has to do when the left-handed pitcher looks at first is break for second — it will give him a great jump.

It's imperative for the coach to see that every pitcher uses the same look both ways.

Runner on Second

It's harder to hold a runner at second base than at first. Many factors have a bearing on this:

- The runner on second can get a much bigger lead.
- Pitchers fall into set patterns more frequently with a runner at second.
- It is harder for a pitcher to develop a good pickoff move to second.

Most runners will try to extend their normal 15-foot lead when they intend to steal third, particularly against pitchers who usually check the runner and then kick and throw to the plate. They'll extend their lead when the pitcher picks up his mitt and then break as soon as the pitcher kicks and delivers.

The smart pitcher will vary his looks to second and his sets to the plate, preventing the runner from reading him.

Another good pitching tactic is to step off the mound, spin, and either hold the baseball or fake a throw. This will let the runner know that the pitcher is aware of him and will also keep the runner from becoming comfortable with his lead and jump.

Photo 1-3   *Photo 1-4*

The pitcher has two basic ways of making his pickoff move:

1) He can whirl toward his gloved-hand side and throw to second (outside pivot).

2) He can whirl and throw (inside pivot). (Photos 1-3 and 1-4)

The inside pivot offers a great change of pace that will catch a lot of runners off the bag. All the pitcher has to do is show this move a few times and the runners will start thinking twice about stealing third.

To steal third, the runner must be able to time the pitcher's rhythm. Pitchers who always use a set rhythm — one-thousand-one, one-thousand-two, then go to the plate — are giving the experienced runner a big invitation to go.

Basically, then, the pitcher can do four things to stop the runner:

1) Vary his looks to second.

2) Vary his time-sets to the plate.

3) Execute an inside pivot to go along with his regular outside pick.

4) Kick to the plate while looking at the runner.

Runner on Third

This is probably the easiest base for the pitcher to control. Very few teams try to steal home. The pitcher (working from his regular stance) will generally check the runner to see what kind of lead he has and whether he is moving or standing still. (Photo 1-5)

He must be trained never to take more than 3.25 seconds to deliver to the plate. He doesn't have to rush, but he cannot be slow or a speedster can steal home on him.

The pitcher must understand that the first thing the runner will look for is a pitcher who doesn't check him. The second thing he will check is the pitcher's delivery time.

If the pitcher has difficulty in these two areas, he can be advised to pitch from a stretch. It's impossible to steal home against a pitcher who works from that position.

Photo 1-5

These are just a few of the techniques that can be used against the running game. Well-prepared teams that like to run will always be able to steal a base or two here and there. The trick is to prevent them from running with any degree of consistency. Defensive teams that get careless against an aggressive running club are going to get stolen blind.

It's important to develop your pitchers' techniques in game-simulated situations. Teach them to focus on both the runner and the plate, and to throw the ball the same way all the time, whether anyone is on base or not.

The coach must set up the game situations and get the pitcher used to holding runners while working on the hitters. He needs all the practice he can get in preparing for teams that run all the time.

Once again: The key to stopping the running game lies in upsetting the runners' timing and making them feel uncomfortable when they take their leads. Bad jumps can be usually converted into big outs.

Pickoff Move

The left-handed pitcher has a distinct advantage over the right-handed pitcher on the pickoff move to first base. He faces the base in his stance on the mound, while the right-handed pitcher has his back to the bag.

Coaches will do well to videotape every pitcher's pickoff moves and show them to the athletes, letting them see exactly what they do when they deliver to the plate and when they go to first for the pickoff.

Left-handed Pitcher

This is probably the best pickoff move in the book. It is based on the imaginary 45-degree line that runs from the mound to a point between first base and home plate. Many umpires will give the left-handed pitcher 4 to 6 inches extra, and the pitcher himself can "cheat" a little more giving him an even better angle for his pickoff move.

The left-handed pitcher starts the move by picking up his leg as if to go to the plate while looking at the runner on first. As his leg comes up, he shifts his vision to the imaginary 45-degree line giving the illusion that he is going to the plate. (Sequence 1-5)

Sequence 1-5

What he is actually doing is driving his lead shoulder at that imaginary 45-degree line. As he plants his foot at that angle, he drops his arm and throws (low three-quarter arm motion) to first base, aiming at the inside of the bag. A quick, accurate throw will often catch the runner extending his lead or taking a jab step toward second base.

The left-handed pitcher can also try to pick off the runner with a quick step-off move from the back part of the rubber, throwing to first with a short, quick sidearm motion.

Right-Handed Pitcher's Pickoff Move

The right-handed pitcher should come to his set position without opening his lead shoulder to see what kind of a lead the runner has. (Photo 1-6) **Warning:** If he opens up his shoulders too much he'll tip off the move to the runner.

Some right-handed pitchers like to use a jump move to first. They will jump off the rubber and turn at the same time, stepping toward first base with the left foot. Note: He must step with the left foot, otherwise it will be a balk.

Grips and Deliveries

Every pitcher has to master at least three pitches — a fastball, some type of breaking ball whether it is a curveball, slider or knuckle, and an outstanding change-up. It is essential to develop a change-up especially if the pitcher doesn't have a good fastball and curveball.

A pitcher can get away with two basic pitches — an outstanding fastball and a great breaking pitch, but it is the third pitch (the change-up) that will take him to the next level.

The pitcher must develop a feel for the baseball. He should hold the ball firmly, without choking it, with his index and middle fingers across the seams. The actual grip will depend on the size of his hands. If he has short, stubby fingers,

Photo 1-6a   *Photo 1-6b*

he will want to hold the ball deeper in his hand. If he has long fingers, he will want to hold the ball farther out in his hand. The center of his fingerprint should be in contact with the seams. Pressure on either finger can cause ball movement.

To break the ball in toward the right-handed hitter, the pitcher should release the middle finger pressure slightly while maintaining firm contact with the index finger. To cause the baseball to break away from the right-handed hitter, the pitcher should release the pressure on the index finger while maintaining firm contact with the middle finger.

Fastball Grip

There are basically two kinds of fastball grips — across the seams, (Photo 1-7) which will produce a rising action, and on the seams, (Photo 1-8) which will produce a sinking movement right to left. The index finger will control the direction of the fastball.

Photo 1-7   *Photo 1-8*

Curveball

The ball should be gripped on a seam or against the seam to get the greatest rotation possible. (Photo 1-9) The fingers should apply firm pressure, but not tight enough to lock the wrist. The deeper the baseball is held in the hand, the greater will be the break on the ball.

The arm motion is exactly the same as for the fastball, right up until the hand reaches the top of the shoulder. At that point, the wrist is sharply snapped to the left (right-handed pitchers), putting the rotation on the ball and the movement down and away.

Note: The motion must be the same as for the fastball to avoid tipping off the curveball.

The ball should come up over the top of the forefinger on the release. The pitcher can practice the action by snapping the ball out of the top of his hand with the thumb and second finger, allowing him to get the best rotation and the best break on the ball.

Photo 1-9

The amount of wrist rotation helps govern the amount of break before it crosses the plate. A certain amount of looseness in the wrist is needed for additional seam rotation. The greater the angle of the wrist, the sharper the break on the ball. The wrist action (snap) should be sharp, not lazy.

The curve can be thrown at various speeds and should be kept low and usually away. We try to have the right-handed pitcher achieve a 1-to-7 o'clock type of wrist action. A 12-to-6 action would be great but few pitchers can do it; it also puts a lot of strain on the elbow.

I have found that many pitchers who throw curveballs tend to hold the ball on the side. I want them to keep their fingers on top of the baseball and pull down while flipping up with the thumb, providing the ultimate rotation on the curveball.

Remember, the arm action is the same as for the fastball — fastball, fastball, fastball, then curve!

The Slider

If not thrown properly, this pitch will put a tremendous amount of strain on the elbow. A good slider will have a short down-and-across break, no more than 2 to 3 inches on either plane.

As previously mentioned, a pitcher with small hands should hold his slider a little deeper in his hand, whereas a pitcher with big hands and long fingers should hold the slider out more in the fingers.

The hand must be kept on top of the baseball so that the release point will be more out in front. (Photo 1-10) This will give the pitcher the best possible chance to cut through the ball and get the proper wrist action.

Photo 1-10

The key to throwing the slider with maximum velocity and minimum elbow strain lies in using the fingers, not the wrist, to spin the baseball.

The fingers should stay on top of the ball as the hand moves to the release point (above the shoulder), where the wrist is snapped and the ball comes off the index finger. The arm must then move across the body in the follow-through.

During this movement, the back of the hand must stay parallel to the ground — preventing the wrist from turning and producing a slow-breaking pitch (more like a slur). The wrist action will put a lot of pressure on the elbow. Remember this when working with young pitchers.

Change-up

This is the most underrated pitch in baseball. I believe it should be taught to pitchers at a very young age, since it is easy on the arm and gives the pitcher two basic pitches — fastball and change-up.

As they grow older, about 13-14, youngsters can begin figuring out how to throw a breaking pitch. At this point in time, the arms and hands will have developed enough to throw the right kind of slider or curveball.

The ideal change-up is thrown about 10 to 15 miles per hour slower than the fastball. This makes the fastball seem faster and forces the hitter to wait longer.

The three-finger grip makes the pitch easy to control. As you can see in Photo 1-11, the pitcher spreads his index, middle and ring fingers across the top of the ball while pinching the pinkie finger and thumb together. This will put the ball deeper in the palm. The pitch is thrown with the same kind of arm speed as the fastball.

Circle Change

This popular change-up pitch derives its name from the position of the thumb and index fingers, which are held together on the inside of the baseball, forming the

Photo 1-11   *Photo 1-12*

shape of a circle. (Photo 1-12) Since this is a very difficult pitch to throw, the pitcher may modify the grip by bringing his index finger up a little and moving the thumb over to the side of the ball making it really a four-finger change-up.

As the pitcher learns to control the pitch, he can gradually bring his index finger and thumb together to get more right-to-left movement.

Some coaches will teach the pitcher how to let his wrist go stiff or "dead" to kill the velocity of the pitch. We want our pitchers to hold the ball out in the fingers and throw it like a fastball with good wrist action.

 ***Coaching Point:*** *The pitcher should never slow up his arm speed, as this will tip off the pitch. To repeat: Make sure the pitcher gets on top of the pitch and throws through the ball, allowing the grip to work for him in killing the ball's velocity.*

Split-Finger Fastball

This was the pitch of the '80s thanks to its guru, Roger Craig.

The ball is simply wedged between the middle finger and index finger so that it will tumble forward out of the hand with forward rotation. (Photo 1-13)

Pitchers with good-sized hands are able to throw the split-finger much easier than pitchers with short, stubby hands who will find it almost impossible to throw it effectively. By gripping the ball out in the fingers, the pitcher can often have the ball float up to the plate, lose velocity, and break downward, causing "the bottom to drop out" of the ball.

Photo 1-13

The thumb is placed directly under the ball, but as a pitcher gets a feel for the pitch he may rotate his thumb to the side of the baseball, causing even more action and a right-to-left action that will make the ball sink.

Fielding

Every pitcher must become an infielder after he releases the baseball. He must be able to pounce on bunted balls and slowly hit balls, catch screaming line drives hit right back at him, and back up third or home.

As mentioned earlier, the pitcher must end each pitch in the proper fielding position — squared off with the plate — so that he can field anything hit up the middle at him.

Any time the pitcher falls off to the side, he not only puts himself in poor position to field a ball, but makes himself vulnerable to line drives hit right back at him.

On bunted balls and swinging bunts down the third-base line, the pitcher must bounce off the mound and put his body in position to field the ball and throw it to a bag.

We teach a no-step fielding position. We want the pitcher to get to the ball and put his center of gravity over it. As he picks it up, he can rock onto his back foot and throw to first without shuffling his feet.

If the ball is hit or bunted sharply to him, giving him the time to handle it, he can, of course, shuffle his feet to ensure the best possible throw to first, as shown in Sequence 1-6.

Sequence 1-6

Fielding Rule

On any ball hit to the right side of the infield, the pitcher must automatically break to first base to cover the bag in case the first baseman has been pulled away.

If time permits, he should race to the foul line about 20 to 25 feet from first and then turn up and race to the bag for the throw from the first or second baseman. This will enable him to avoid contact with the runner and turn back quickly toward the infield for a possible play on another runner.

Communication is extremely important. If the pitcher can get to the ball, he should yell, "Ball! Ball!" to get the first baseman to break back to the bag. On a ball he cannot field, he should yell, "Take it! Take it!" and continue on to cover the bag.

On infield fly balls that can be fielded by two or more players, the pitcher should yell the name of the player he feels is in the best position to make the catch.

Great mechanics can make a fifth infielder out of the pitcher and help him tack a few extra W's onto his record. He should never take his fielding for granted. He should work on the various plays in practice.

The big, big point in pitching and defense in general is:

Never give the offense an extra out.

2
Catcher

A good catcher is worth his weight in gold to a baseball team. Among the attributes a good catcher will possess:

- Leadership.
- The ability to take charge.
- Sound fundamentals.

Good catchers can be an enormous help to a pitching staff.

Every good catcher is a leader and spark plug of the ballclub. He handles the pitchers and helps run the infield. He must also be quick and have the agility not only to catch pitches but also get out on top of bunts and other balls hit just in front of the plate. A catcher who can do all these things can be forgiven for limitations on offense.

A catcher has several defensive responsibilities — catching pop-ups, backing up first on occasion and, of course, fielding the position. The old adage that if you are strong up the middle you are strong, starts with the catcher. He must be able to throw and receive the baseball, and block pitches in the dirt in key situations.

The catcher's job became much easier in the 1970s when Johnny Bench made the single break mitt popular. It allowed catchers to catch the ball with one hand. Until that time, catchers had to use the no-break or no-hinge glove that required both hands to consistently catch the ball. Although there is now a double break mitt in use, the single break is still the most popular.

Hitters take special care of their bats and other fielders do the same with their gloves. Catchers must do the same with their equipment — shin guards, chest protector and mask. These are the tools of the catcher's trade and should not go unprotected.

The shin guards and chest protector should fit snugly and give maximum protection. The mask may be made of either metal or a plastic material. The metal mask gives the catcher a better view and covers the ears a little bit better. The plastic is lighter but doesn't have the visual benefits of the metal mask.

17

The shin guards should be strapped to the outside and cover the leg adequately from the toe all the way up to the lower thigh area. It is important that the catcher use protective head gear that is either attached to the mask, or a batting helmet that can be worn backward.

Giving Signs

When giving the signs, the catcher must be in a stance that provides the pitcher with an unimpeded view yet doesn't allow base coaches or runners at first and third base to see them. The glove helps protect the signs from the eyes of the third base coach. The glove should be placed on the outside of the knee which will block any view from the third base area. The catcher should spread his fingers and keep them in the back against the crotch area. Fingers too low or too high will be able to be seen from the on deck circle or by the base coaches. (Photo 2-1)

There are many systems for giving signs to the pitchers and middle infielders. Keep it simple so that the pitchers and middle infielders are not crossed but difficult enough to keep a runner at second from picking up the signs and relaying them to the hitters. Usually with no one on base, most catchers will just give one sign. One is a fastball, two is a curve, three is a slider, four is a change-up, or it can be given in reverse order.

With a runner at second base, more than one sign must be given. If not, the offense will develop a system to relay it to the hitter letting him know what pitch is coming. There are a lot of things that you can do. It can be the first sign after the catcher putting down two fingers, it can be the last sign, the first sign, one pump, two pumps or vary with outs. There are many different ways to camouflage what pitch is coming.

It is important that every team have two sets of signs. If you feel the offense has picked

Photo 2-1

up your signs at second base, you can go to your second set. It is also important to practice both sets throughout the year so that the defense is comfortable with the second set. Also, we don't want our catchers squatting in the middle of the plate to give signs and then moving to one corner or the other. This would give the batter and the coaches some indication as to what pitch is coming.

If the catcher is calling the game and not getting signs from the dugout, then he should have an idea as to what pitch is coming and set up outside or inside to give the sign. This would also help camouflage whether we are going in or out. After giving the sign and going into the setup position, he can set up inside and move to the outside just before the pitcher finishes his windup which also confuses the offense as to whether a pitch is coming inside or outside.

Photo 2-2   *Photo 2-3*

After giving the sign, the catcher should set up in the stance dictated by whether there are runners on base or not. The feet should be shoulder width apart, right toe lined up with the left instep. The catcher is now in a position to throw and field with his weight on the inside of his ankles. (Photo 2-2)

With runners on base, the catcher simply raises up his tail slightly to allow him to block pitches better, shift quickly and throw to second with more ease and accuracy. It is essential that the catcher give the pitcher a good target by pointing his fingers toward the pitcher with the pocket actually facing the ground. This helps emphasize a low target.

The catcher must to be careful not to get the elbow inside the left shin guard which will lock him out on an inside pitch. He wants to reach out with his arms slightly bent allowing him enough flexibility to catch the ball in any direction. Also, with no one on base, the catcher wants to protect his bare hand from any foul tips by putting it right behind the right knee.

With a runner on base, some catchers position their bare hand behind the catcher's mitt not only for added protection, but also to make them a little quicker in stealing situations. (Photo 2-3) If a catcher is comfortable with this method he should tuck the thumb lightly inside and make a fist which keeps the thumb from being hit with a foul tip.

Receiving

The catcher is involved with more defensive plays than any other player on the field. Just think about it. Every catcher will receive more than 100 pitches in a game, so receiving the baseball is probably his most important job. His skill factor must be impeccable.

But another important factor is a catcher's ability to turn one or two borderline pitches each inning into strikes. Using the proper technique, a catcher can turn 10 to

Photo 2-4   *Photo 2-5*

15 pitches that could be called either way into strikes. This will add up by the end of the game and make a big difference in the outcome.

A catcher must learn how to quarter turn when the pitcher releases the baseball. At this point, the catcher must simply turn the thumb straight up as in Photos 2-4 and 2-5 which puts his glove in a position that now requires only a 90-degree turn. If the catcher keeps his fingers pointing straight ahead, he must turn 180 degrees to catch a low pitch. Quarter turning also frees the wrist giving the catcher more flexibility and the ability to receive the ball with much more ease.

We use the phrase "framing the pitch" when we want our catchers to cup the ball, frame it or round it off by catching the outside of the ball out in front with a slightly extended arm. This gives the umpire the best possible view. We want to try and catch a ball that is 3 inches out of the strike zone, cup it in and round it off to give the illusion that it is on the corner and in a position to be called a strike by the umpire. We are trying to cut the glove 2 to 3 inches down, in or up, making the pitch look closer to the plate than it really is.

In framing the pitch, the catcher must catch the ball out in front by extending his arm and actually sticking the ball. I have found that balls 4 to 5 inches off the plate which the catcher can make look a little closer give the umpire the sense that the pitcher really isn't that wild and keeps everything right around the plate. This gives an illusion that the pitcher has been around the plate all day.

A catcher who uses the proper technique can make his pitcher look good, but using improper technique can make a pitcher look like he is much wilder than he really is.

Pitch Down the Middle of the Plate

On a pitch right over the plate, the catcher simply gives slightly and cups the ball up and in toward his body without moving and disturbing the umpire's concentration or view. Notice in Photos 2-6 and 2-7 how the catcher receives the ball right down the middle and cups it in with very little movement.

When catching an inside pitch, it is important for the catcher to keep his glove elbow up and above his left knee which allows him to receive the pitch without

Photo 2-7

catches
p down
ing the

ses the ball, the catcher will quarter turn, and reach out
ball, cupping it in as shown in Photo 2-8.

n, he must reach down and catch the sinking fastball or
nded pitcher, sticking it and catching the ball up, and
to 2-9. If the pitch is 5 to 6 inches off the plate and is
wants to sway and reach outside to catch the outside of
hough it is a ball, but it gives the illusion to the umpire
t that far off the plate.

p using
other is
ing it in

and 2-11 how the catcher sways and catches the outside
k much closer than it really is.

turn the
e you to
mes that
the low

)

side Pitch

right must be caught with the backhand technique. The
outside of the ball by rotating his glove and sticking the

Photo 2-9

Photo 2-10　　　　　　　　　*Photo 2-11*

In Photos 2-12 and 2-13 the catcher quarter turns, and reaches out ᵃ the ball. He sticks it and catches it up, and does not allow his mitt to toward the ground. Notice that he sways a little toward his right leg, umpire a good look. This allows him to frame the pitch as he catches it.

Catching the Low Pitch

There are two ways to catch the low pitch. One is cupping the ba your wrist, and rotating the glove 90 degrees and catching the ball up. T catching the ball with fingers pointing down and cupping it up while fun toward the chest.

Different umpires like different techniques. Some like for you to c glove over, rotate the glove 180 degrees and catch the ball up. Others funnel it up the curveball and slider from a left-handed pitcher. I find many quarter turning and catching the ball up gives the umpire a better view pitch down and in to a right-hander or away from a left-hander. (Photo 2

Photo 2-12　　　　　　　　*Photo 2-13*

When catching a high pitch, it is very important to catcher the top of the baseball. On a pitch that is going to be mask high, he needs to make sure that he gets above the ball and cups the glove downward using his wrist.

Remember, every pitch in the strike zone should be caught with a minimum amount of body movement. On pitches outside the strike zone, left or right, the catcher is going to have to sway a little to reach out and catch a ball that is off the plate 6 to 7 inches. The catcher who is able to frame the pitch will get more marginal pitches for his pitcher.

Blocking Pitches

That's why a good stance is essential. A toe-to-instep alignment provides a comfortable and utilitarian base. It enables the catcher to stay low, keep his weight over the balls of his feet, and move quickly and efficiently. Check the stance in the accompanying photo sequences. Note that the catcher's toes are not pointing straight ahead, but out.

The catcher can use one of three positions in his starting stance. He can set up directly behind the plate, inside or outside. It depends on the type of pitch he calls for and where he wants it.

For example, if he calls for a curveball with a right-hander on the mound, he'll want to set up a little outside to allow for the break and be in better position to block the ball if it's in the dirt. With a left-hander on the mound, he'll want to set up a little inside.

Coaching Point: *At the higher levels of the game, most fastball pitchers won't throw many pitches more than a foot off the plate, so the catcher can set up more directly behind the plate. It's the curveball pitchers who tend to get the ball extra wide or inside.*

Sequence 2-1

A lot of coaches discourage their catchers from setting up directly behind the plate. They want them to shade to the outside or inside, except when the count goes 3-0 or 2-0. The shaded position gives the pitcher a better target on the corner and helps the catcher go out (or in) for the extreme pitch.

In blocking pitches directly behind the plate, the catcher must avoid the tendency to lay back unaggressively. He must attack the baseball, cutting down the distance between himself and the ball. This will keep the ball from bouncing over him.

As soon as the catcher sees the ball bouncing into the dirt, he should fall forward to his knees, as shown in Sequence 2-1, and drop his glove and open hand to the ground directly in front of him. Remember, the idea is to block the ball, not catch it.

As you can see, the toed-out stance enables the catcher to sit down on his heels and get lower to the ground while the glove-and-hand position prevents the ball from going through the gap between the legs.

The elbows are kept close to the body to prevent any holes for the ball to slip through. The shoulders are slightly rounded and the upper body leans forward so that the ball will bounce off the chest and fall in front of the body. The chin is tucked in on the chest to protect the throat from a high bounce.

Typical mistakes in blocking a pitch:

- Not getting the glove and open hand down on the ground between the legs.
- Not reacting quickly enough.
- Not sitting on the heels, which makes for a bigger area to cover with the glove-and-hand position.
- Turning the upper body toward first base, which allows the ball to rebound off the chest toward the foul side of the first-base line.
- Flinching.

Note: The catcher must try to block the ball back in the direction it came from. As long as he can keep the ball in front of him, he has a chance of keeping the runners from advancing.

Sequence 2-2

Sequence 2-3

The ball that bounces about 6 to 8 inches off the plate can be blocked the same way as the ball directly behind the plate. Sequences 2-2 and 2-3 show the catcher blocking pitches about 6 to 8 inches to the right and left of the plate.

The catcher must be a little quicker on these pitches and must round the ball off a little by positioning his body so that the ball rebounds off his chest in front of him. If he doesn't round the ball, it could bounce off his body and roll down either foul line, allowing the runner to advance.

The ball that hits more than a foot off the plate has to be blocked a different way. When anticipating a pitch to his right, the catcher should place a little more weight on his left foot. This will make him a little quicker in getting the right foot out to block the ball.

In Sequence 2-4, the catcher steps out with his right foot and then sits down on his right knee while extending his left leg with the inside of the heel down.

Sequence 2-4

Also notice how:

1) He covers up the hole between his legs with the glove and free hand.

2) He leans his upper body forward.

3) He tucks in his chin and rounds his shoulders.

4) He rounds the ball to keep it from kicking off to the side.

Sequence 2-5: The catcher does everything the same when he goes left, except with different limbs. He starts by placing a little more weight on his right foot, which allows him to be quicker in getting the left leg out to block the pitch. He then sits down on his knee, allowing his right let to extend out on the heel of the foot. Again he rounds the ball very well.

Sequence 2-5

Notice the importance of keeping the elbows in, not out. The catcher is making a successful play because his right arm is tucked in. Notice the ball bouncing up into the juncture of the chest and forearm. There is no hole for the ball to get through.

Another important point that must be made here concerns blocking the curveball. On a right-hander's curveball, the catcher must position himself so that the right shoulder just covers the outside of the ball. (See Sequence 2-4.) The spin would then cause the ball to kick back a little toward the left shoulder.

If the catcher positions his body directly in front of the ball, the spin would cause the ball to kick back and bounce by his left shoulder.

On a left-hander's curveball, the catcher's left shoulder must be in position to just cover the ball, allowing for the kickback from the spin. (Sequence 2-5)

This technique enables the catcher to:

• Be quicker in getting outside on a ball in the dirt.

• Cover more ground.

• Come up into a throwing position much faster.

Fielding Bunts

Defense covers a variety of areas from catching pop-ups, backing up third base on occasion and, of course, fielding the position. The catcher must be able to pounce on anything tapped or bunted in front of the plate, which means that he must have quick feet.

Ball Bunted Down Third-Base Line

If the ball stops in the dirt, the catcher can round it off, never losing sight of first base. He also has a decision to make on this play. If the ball rolls to the grass, he must shed his mask (so that it won't get in his way), stay low and trail the ball.

Sequence 2-6 shows the catcher getting over the ball and scooping it into his mitt, which assures him of picking it up. The catcher should avoid trying to barehand the ball which often results in failure to control it.

After scooping up the ball, the catcher must concentrate on squaring up his shoulders for his throw to first, as shown in Sequence 2-7. He points the lead shoulder in the direction he intends to throw. The shoulder is like a gun sight, and the catcher wants to put it right on the target.

Sequence 2-6

Sequence 2-7

The throw should be made overhand because it offers the most accuracy. If time is of the essence, the catcher can throw sidearm or underhand right from the crouch, making sure the throw doesn't tail into the runner.

Ball Bunted Down First-Base Line

This kind of ball can be fielded in two ways with the catcher considering the following factors:

1) How fast is the runner?

2) How hard is the ball hit?

Sequence 2-8 shows the play on a bunt that just makes it into the grassy area of the field. This gives the catcher time to scoop it up with his mitt and square up to throw to first. After scooping the ball, the catcher must shuffle a little off the line to

27

Sequence 2-8

get a better angle for the throw to avoid hitting the runner. The catcher has gotten rid of his mask early, flipping it behind him where it won't interfere with the play. After squaring up, he throws to the infield side of the bag.

Sequence 2-9 shows the play on a ball bunted farther down the line. The catcher's first two steps are again toward the mound, enabling him to round off the ball and get into position for the throw to first.

Sequence 2-9

Since the catcher doesn't have time to square up for the throw, he must throw from down low to the infield side of first. He must also put a 12-6 rotation on the ball instead of a 9-3 rotation. A 9-3 rotation will cause the ball to tail into the runner in this situation.

The 12-6 rotation can be achieved by keeping the fingers under the ball and the wrist parallel to the legs. Obviously, some players won't be able to adjust to this throwing technique. If the catcher is successful with a 9-3 rotation, don't change it.

Strike Three, Ball in the Dirt

With less than two outs and first base unoccupied, a hitter can run to first on a third strike not caught by the catcher. With two outs, the batter can run to first even is it is occupied if the catcher fails to catch the ball on a third strike.

Because of this rule it is important for the catcher to block the ball in the dirt, keeping his legs together and his mitt on the ground to prevent the ball from going under him.

As a rule, the ball will rebound off the catcher either foul or fair. If the ball rebounds into foul territory, the catcher must get rid of his mask, go after the ball and scoop it up with the mitt.

He must square his shoulders up with first and throw to the foul side of the bag. The first baseman should help by yelling, "Outside! Outside!" If the ball pops out in front of the plate, the catcher should go out, scoop it up and throw to the infield side of first, as the first baseman yells "Inside! Inside!"

> **Coaching Point:** *The catcher must remember to shuffle out away from the line to get a better angle for his throw to first.*

Throwing

Catchers basically have to do two things well:

1) Receive the baseball.

2) Be able to throw out runners.

It is no secret that they must get help from the pitcher. When you show up for practice and the pitcher throws 2.0 it isn't going to get any better on game day. A pitcher has got to be somewhere around 1.3 seconds to the plate from the time he moves to the time the ball hits the catcher's mitt.

There are basically two things that allow the catcher to throw accurately and with consistency. One is the exchange of the ball from the glove to the throwing hand, and the other is the footwork of the lower body. Both are essential in being consistent in throwing out runners in an adequate time.

Jump Pivot Method

This is probably the most popular method in throwing the baseball to second base. Catchers with quick feet usually use this technique on a ball thrown right down the middle of the plate. As the ball hits the mitt he quickly shifts his feet, pointing his shoulder toward second base with his right foot pointing toward the first-base dugout. (Sequence 2-10) He will then step and transfer his weight to his left foot finishing his throw to second base.

On balls that are left or right the catcher must use the step-and-throw technique, stepping with the right foot and then planting and throwing to second base.

Sequence 2-10

Jab Step Method

The jab step method is recommended for catchers with average throwing strength. Just before receiving a pitch that is in the middle of the plate the catcher will jab step 6 to 8 inches with his right foot to gain momentum toward second base. (Sequence 2-11) He must turn his right foot perpendicular to second base so that he can rotate his hips and shoulders. This allows him to align his lead shoulder toward second base, which puts him in a good position to release the ball. He will need to follow through with his left foot, transferring his weight as he releases the baseball.

For balls on the inside corner, the catcher will jab step with his left foot first, receive the ball and then readjust his feet similar to the jump pivot method allowing him to be in position to throw to second base.

Sequence 2-11

Notice in Sequence 2-11 on a pitch on the outside part of the plate he will jab step with his right foot to receive it, turn his shoulders and rotate toward second base, and follow through by transferring his weight to his lead foot as he completes the throw. The key here is to make sure his momentum is going toward second base and not first as he releases the ball to second.

Rocker Step Method

The next method is for catchers who have strong arms. As he receives the ball, the catcher rocks back on his right foot, rotates his shoulders, steps and throws to second base on pitch down the middle of the plate. (Sequence 2-12) This is probably the quickest way to release the baseball, but you must possess a very strong arm. There are few catchers able to use this technique.

Sequence 2-12

Catching Pop-ups

Any time a ball is popped up in foul territory directly behind the catcher, it has backspin on it. As it descends, the ball will drift back toward the infield. The catcher must keep this in mind as he prepares to catch the pop-up.

He must first remove his mask and find the ball. Then he should turn his back to the infield and get in a position to catch it, whether he has to move 6 to 10 feet away from home plate or simply catch the ball right around the home plate area. As he locates the ball and gets near it, he must toss his mask to the right allowing him to catch the ball with two hands as in Sequence 2-13.

Notice that the catcher does not release the mask until he has located the ball and is in position to catch it. Then he simply tosses the mask off to the right, reaches up and catches the ball above his head using two hands. The key is to remember the ball will drift back toward the infield. Make sure you don't overrun it and allow the ball to drift back over your head.

Sequence 2-13

There are also times where you are going to have to sprint for the ball and it is going to be a bang-bang play at the wall or in the bat rack or even the dugout. Here the catcher can use the bent-leg slide to avoid injuring himself and use his protective gear (shin guards especially) to aid in catching the baseball. Notice in Sequence 2-14 that the catcher uses the bent-leg slide in catching the ball right up against the wall which gives him a little added protection. The bent-leg technique should only be used on balls that are not hit very high.

Sequence 2-14

Tag Plays

When receiving the throw from a cutoff man or from the outfield the catcher wants to set up in front of the plate giving the runner the back part of the plate to slide to. This allows the catcher to know exactly where the runner is going to be as he receives the baseball. He is going to stand on the front part of the plate with his left foot, shin guard and toes pointing up the third-base line and face the play with his body whether the throw comes from left field, center field or right field. He must keep his left foot positioned so his shin guards are pointing toward third base which helps him avoid injury from a runner sliding into his left leg.

Sequence 2-15

As he receives the throw, he will step with his left foot, taking the plate away while he goes to his right knee into position to block the plate, keeping the runner from making contact with it. At the same time, he uses his bare hand to cover the baseball with all four fingers as in Sequence 2-15. He tags the runner and then pulls the ball out to show it to the umpire.

In conclusion, you can see that the catcher is the glue that holds the defense together. He is involved in every single pitch that is thrown in the game.

3
Infield Play

Most action in baseball occurs in the infield. Normally, nine or 10 putouts are credited to the outfield during a game. The rest, obviously, result from strikeouts, groundouts, pop-ups or sacrifices.

An infielder's amazing grab or the pinpoint timing of a double play can keep a team alive. So you can see that good infielders are worth their weight in gold.

Ready Position

The proper stance is one of the most important aspects for an infielder when preparing to catch a ground ball. It should be a comfortable position with the feet a little more than shoulder-width apart and slightly staggered. (Photo 3-1) Also notice the position of the hands. They are in front and relaxed with palms facing each other.

In this position, the infielder must make only a one-quarter or 90-degree turn to catch a ground ball or turn the glove the other way to catch a line drive. Remember, though, that most middle infielders will have to move more than a couple of steps up, back or sideways in order to catch a ground ball or line drive. The elbows should be in close to the body instead of out. The wrists should also be relaxed.

In Photo 3-2 the infielder is crouched over with his glove open out in front. This puts him in good position to catch a ball hit right at him, but it does not allow him to get a good jump on a ball that would require him to move five steps to his left. The main reason is that some infielders tend to spread their feet too wide and start too low to the ground. I prefer an infielder to start out a little higher. Again, it is a personal preference as is the jump or lack of jump that the infielder is able to achieve from that position.

Some infielders like to take a couple of jab steps as the pitcher winds up and releases the ball. This gives the player a little movement and keeps him from getting stiff and having dead feet.

Photos 3-3 and 3-4 show the proper method of moving the right foot and then the left.

Photo 3-1

Photo 3-2

Photo 3-3

Photo 3-4

Photo 3-5   *Photo 3-6*

Here he is toe-to-toe. He feels comfortable here and is in great position to move either left or right. If a player staggers his feet, it should be in a right toe-to-instep of the left foot relationship.

Photos 3-5 and 3-6 illustrate how the feet are out of position. A ball hit sharply to his right will make it difficult to achieve the angle necessary to catch the ball. He is also a little too low and the glove hand could become stiff in this position if he isn't careful.

I believe in teaching players good glove position, but remember not to have the players open it too soon and pointing it at the hitter before the ball is hit. This causes the hands to become locked out and stiff. The hands needs to be relaxed and loose.

Excellent glove position in the ready phase of the stance is shown in Photos 3-4 and 3-5. Glove position is essential in catching the ground ball, but the infielder must remain relaxed and natural when he is in the stance.

Reading Pitches to Get a Jump on the Ball

A part of the stance that is often overlooked is tracking the ball from the pitcher to the plate. Good infielders move after the ball has been hit. Excellent infielders move before it has been hit.

For example, if a fastball is thrown in to a pull hitter and he starts to turn on the pitch, the great infielder anticipates this and starts to move to his right. In a similar situation, if the pitcher throws a hanging curveball the hitter is more likely to pull this pitch. Again, the great infielder gets an excellent jump toward his right by reading the movement of the hitter.

Another situation may find a right-handed hitter who hits well to all fields and gets an outside pitch. Reading the body actions of the hitter can tell the fielder where the ball is likely to be hit. If the hitter stays behind the ball well, he is more likely to drive the ball to right field or to the right side of the diamond.

If the hitter is fooled by an off-speed pitch and lunges at the ball or tries to pull the pitch because he is in front, the fielder will read this immediately. The great infielder anticipates and gets an excellent jump.

How do you improve on reading hitters? At practice, of course! The best time is while the coach is throwing batting practice. Track the ball from the mound to the plate. Watch the hitter to see how he reacts on certain pitches. Does he bail out, stay behind the ball, open up? Try to anticipate where the ball is going to be hit. Is it going to be hit right at you, or to your left or right? Also, how hard is the ball hit? If hit sharply, you will have to take a deeper angle.

It is equally important to add information to your computer system as you track the ball. Feed in additional information such as:

1) Type of pitcher (junk or fastball)

2) Pitch that is to be thrown

3) Condition of ground (hard or soft)

4) How hard the ball is hit

5) Speed of the runner

All of this will help give you the information you need to get the best possible jump.

Catching a Ball Hit Directly at the Fielder

Sequence 3-1 shows great glove position. As the fielder approaches the ball, his glove is open out in front with his meat hand above the glove. The ball is caught in front of, not underneath, his body. Fielding the ball under him creates a blind spot — he cannot see the last bounce into the glove.

Sequence 3-1

Photo 3-7   *Photo 3-8*

Photo 3-7 shows the great glove position. Notice the knees are at a 90-degree angle. Bending the knees causes the glove to extend in front of the body. You can't field a ball consistently by standing up.

Infielders, remember these three rules when catching a ground ball:

1) Bend at the waist.

2) Bend at the knees.

3) Get the glove on the ground out in front as in Photo 3-8.

Remember, if you start with the glove on the ground you only have to move it one direction on a bad hop — up.

Let's look at sequence 3-1 one more time. Notice where the bill of the cap is just before the fielder catches the ball. It is pointing down. He has followed the ball all the way into his glove. How often do you see an infielder boot a ground ball and then not be able to find it?

One of two problems will cause this:

1) The glove wasn't out in front, or

2) He didn't watch the ball into the glove.

If the infielder tracks the ball all the way with proper technique, he will often make the adjustment on a bad hop and catch the ball. Even if he drops the ball, he will at least know where it is and be able to pick it up for a possible throw to first base. This is especially true at second base where the second baseman still has a play even if he bobbles the ball.

Catching the Ball

I want to emphasize that the players need to play the ball instead of letting the ball play them. Don't get caught back on your heels. In that position, your chances of catching the ball consistently are greatly reduced.

Be aggressive! I prefer the phrase, "Approach the baseball" rather than "Charge the baseball" because a charging player may seem out of control.

People talk about how great an infielder's hands are. While hands are definitely important, the most important quality for an infielder is good, quick feet. You catch and throw the baseball with your feet. By that I mean your feet get your body in either a good or bad position to catch the baseball. Don't get me wrong, an infielder must also possess good soft hands. You can have great feet and hands of steel and be the worst infielder. But, if you have adequate hands and great feet, you can become a pretty good infielder.

The hands and feet should be the two main ingredients that an infielder tries to develop. The hands are very important to the infielder. With a good pair of hands, he can make a tough play look easy. Your goal as an infielder should be to develop soft hands.

As you approach the ball take short, choppy steps 5 to 6 feet away from where you are going to catch the ball. Sequence 3-1 shows that as he approaches the ball he is not patting the glove or having the back of the glove facing the ball. His first essential step is somewhat big but then the steps begin to get smaller.

Look at the great glove position after he has taken his second step. It is more natural and fluid this way instead of having the glove open, facing the hitter in the ready position and then approaching the ball. Many times this creates stiff, unnatural hand action.

The approach should be similar to an airplane killing its engine and gliding into the runway. This method eliminates the herky-jerky, last-minute fielding action.

Sequence 3-1 shows him bending at the knees and waist. He does not bend strictly from the waist as many young infielders do. As he extends his arms to catch the ball out in front, it causes his buttocks to become lower, putting him in a great fielding position. This gives his hands room to give a little after catching the ball much like a shock absorber. Keep in mind that while catching the ball out in front, it enables you to give a little. Here you can see the slightly staggered toe-to-instep position. This gives the player good balance.

The glove position before the ball enters the glove is of utmost concern. The fingers are pointing directly toward the ball. The glove should be angled on the same plane as the forearm. The web of the glove should be touching the ground. If the fingers are pointing directly into the ground then the wrist is locked out and the result will be a stiff wrist and hand instead of the desired soft hands.

As the player catches the ball, the meat hand should be above the glove (palm facing palm) so as the ball enters the glove he can reach in and cover the ball.

Another common fault is flattening the glove which causes the fingers to come off the ground. This will cause the ball to hit the fingers of the glove or the back of the heel and pop out.

The two biggest problems young players face are failing to bend their knees and not catching the ball out in front. They either catch the ball to the side or under their bodies and do it while standing up (bending at the waist only).

The body needs to be low when catching a ground ball. As you catch the ball and bring the glove toward your belly button, you are emphasizing a full fluid motion that carries into the throw. This allows the infielder to be very smooth as he approaches the ball, catches it and then throws it in a fluid motion.

Short Hops

Sometimes players get caught in between and get a short hop. The method used to catch the short hop is basically the same except for the glove action.

Notice in Photos 3-8 and 3-9 that the player goes forward with the glove to catch the ball. If he tries to give and bring the glove backward, the ball will hit the heel of the glove, bounce off his arms or go through his legs. This technique cuts down the angle and allows the ball to be caught. It can also be used on backhand and forehand plays.

Photo 3-8   *Photo 3-9*

 Coaching point: *Many times a player will have to approach the ball using good feet in order to get a short hop, which happens to be the best hop he could get on that particular ground ball.*

Again, in Photos 3-8 and 3-9, he has excellent glove, feet, arms, head and body positioning. This is the secret to becoming a consistent infielder.

Throwing

Major-league players today throw overhand, sidearm or underhand depending on where they get the ball. If they get the ball low they don't always have time to come up and throw. But a young ballplayer should throw the ball overhand or three-quarter whenever possible. This is your truest throw. When you throw sidearm, it is hard to control and to catch.

The key to throwing is using your whole body, not just your arm. I believe the reason so many young players get sore arms is their failure to use their whole body. Point your shoulder in the direction you intend to throw. This enables you to use your whole body, not just your arm.

Lateral Movement

In most situations, infielders will have to move up, back, left or right to get into position to catch a ground ball. As mentioned earlier, being able to read the ball off the bat helps the infielder get there a little quicker.

In Sequence 3-2 you can see he is taking a jab step and then a crossover step while opening his hips in order to move to his left. Again he has gotten his glove in excellent position to receive the ball.

A key point when moving to the left or right is to stay low to the ground. Too many times a young infielder's first movement is to stand straight up before moving right or left. The one fluid motion is repeated here in this sequence.

The next sequence (3-3) illustrates the same technique; a short jab step to help open up and then an immediate crossover step with his left foot. Again, as he squares up to the ball, he must have good glove position.

Sequence 3-2

You can see that he has taken a couple of short, quick steps to round the ball off so after he catches the ball his momentum is going toward first base as he starts to throw the ball. The crow-hop here is a short step with his right foot over and in front of his left.

A common fault of many infielders is catching the ball deeper than this player did, causing the body weight to shift toward left field. Now they have to shift back toward first with a herky-jerky method while the runner speeds down the base path.

Sequence 3-3

Forehand Play

There are times when an infielder will have to catch the ball to the side instead of in front of his body. The forehand play can be a real rally killer, but the infielder should only use the forehand when he can't get in front of the ball.

The angle and approach to the ball depend on how hard the ball is hit. The surface also is a factor. High grass will slow the ball's speed but low-cut grass allows it to move a little faster.

In Sequence 3-4 the infielder will move to his left in a straight line. Here he rotates on his left foot while crossing over with his right. Immediately he has good glove position and remains low to the ground. Notice the glove position as he catches the ball. The head is in excellent position. The glove is in front of his left foot, and his knees are bent to give him stability and great technique.

After catching the ball he gives a little with the glove to soften his hands. He brings the glove up to his meat hand in preparing to throw. Look how quickly he gets his feet under him, allowing him to get rid of the ball faster. As I mentioned earlier, a characteristic of a good infielder is quick feet.

The next sequence (3-5) shows that he now has to take a drop step with his left foot in order to get the proper angle to catch the ball. Again, as he crosses over he begins to open his glove as he approaches the ball. Here again you see why great feet make the difference for infielders. He is able to get his feet under him so he can make

Sequence 3-4

the easy throw to first base. I find that many second basemen fail to drop step and take a deep angle back into the grass. Many times they will move straight to their left, never leaving the infield and not even coming close to catching the ball. Remember, you will still have time to throw the runner out at first.

Sequence 3-5

Also think of this situation: Man on second and a ground ball is hit hard to the second baseman's left. If he takes a deep angle he can keep the runner from scoring. If the ball gets by him, it's a run!

There is one play that requires a shallow angle to retrieve a hard-hit ball. Here in Sequence 3-6, he takes a drop step with his left foot in order to get the proper angle needed. After he catches the ball, he does a reverse pivot, adjusts his feet, and throws to first base, all in one motion.

This play can also be used by a third baseman or shortstop. It allows the infielder to get rid of the ball more quickly and, more often than not, put a little more on the throw.

Sequence 3-6

Backhand Play

The backhand play is probably the toughest for an infielder, but it can be a real game-saver. How hard the ball is hit will determine the angle that the infielder must take to reach the ball. If the ball is hit hard, a drop step may be required. If slowly hit, a direct approach is best.

If it is hit at medium speed the player will jab step with his left foot as he crosses over with his right foot (Sequence 3-7) and catches the ball just in front of his left knee. This position will allow him to hook the ball into his glove much more easily. There are two ways to catch the ball with the backhand technique. One is with the right leg extended. This is when the player has to backhand the ball but is under control and able to plant, catch the ball, rotate his hips, and then throw.

In Sequence 3-7 he catches the ball, bringing his thumb and little finger together to form a deep pocket. So many times you will see the ball hit the heel or palm of the glove and bounce out. The infielder should try to catch the ball in the web.

The other method is to catch the ball with the left foot extended. Some infielders like this because they can open their hips and get more power into their throw. Also, the momentum may cause the infielder to catch the ball with the left foot extended and then plant the right foot to get the throw off. However, the nature of the play could cause the infielder to catch with either leg extended.

The extended leg needs to be flexed to allow the infielder to get his glove on the ground. Again, the proper method is to start from the ground up. This will also give the infielder a worm's-eye view, allowing him to adjust to any bad hop.

Sequence 3-7

If the ball happens to be hit a little harder, then a drop step crossover method is needed. Here the left leg is extended as he catches the ball but his momentum carries him to get more on his throw.

However, if his momentum carries him to his right foot then a long step is required to help brace, or brake, his momentum and allow him to get the throw off. If he takes a short step then he will end up taking a couple of steps before he throws the ball.

Whenever you use the backhand method, the glove must lead the way. As he crosses over, the glove goes in front of his left leg to start to get in the proper position. Again, he catches the ball in front while watching the ball go into the glove.

45-Degree Angles

Many times infielders will find it necessary to take a 45-degree angle either to their left or right in order to intercept the ball at the quickest moment. The speed of the runner often plays a major role.

The infielder who waits on the ball will often get a bad hop. Remember, you play the ball, don't let the ball play you. The playing surface may require you to approach the ball more quickly in order to get the runner.

With the proper angles, you can add range to your infield play, but it takes grounder after grounder to perfect it.

4
First Base

There was a time when a first baseman could hit the ball out of the ballpark but wasn't necessarily agile or quick. The trend in recent years, however, is toward first basemen who may not have great power but can play superb defense. A first baseman who can do both is a real gem.

The first baseman who can save runs by scooping the ball out of the dirt on a throw from an infielder, aid in cutoff plays, hop on bunts and throw out lead runners, and makes the great defensive plays is just as valuable to his team as the one who can hit home runs.

Ideally, we would like for the first baseman to be at least 6 feet tall to provide an easy-to-see target for the other infielders. Also, a left-handed first baseman has an easier time on tag plays against runners diving back to first base, and allows the first baseman with the glove on his right hand to cover a little more ground when going to his right. It also helps him on throws to second base when starting the double play with a runner on first.

A great defensive first baseman needs to have quick feet and be able to move around the bag on throws from the middle infielders. He must be able to stretch out and catch that throw on a bang-bang play.

Receiving Throws at First Base

With no one on base, we want our first baseman to be as far off the bag as he possibly can, yet be able to get to the base in time to take throws on balls hit to the infielders. This allows him to cover the most ground possible.

If he happens to be playing a left-handed hitter he might be a little closer to the line which would allow him to get to the bag a little quicker. He might want to play deeper on hitters that do not bunt or drag down the first-base line. If he is facing a hitter who likes to bunt or push the ball down the first-base line, then he must move in a few steps in order to have the opportunity to make that play by flipping the ball to the pitcher covering first base.

On any ground ball to the other infielders, the first baseman must go directly to the base, position his heels on the corner and be ready to take the throw. He wants to square up his shoulders toward the position the throw is coming from.

Once he determines the flight and trajectory of the baseball, he should stretch to the ball. In Sequence 4-1, the ball is thrown directly at the first baseman. As a result, he stretches directly to it.

Sequence 4-1

Timing is important. If he stretches too soon, the ball may go over his head. Make sure of the trajectory before stretching to it.

> **Coaching Point:** *Many young first basemen will stretch before the ball is thrown or before they see the flight of the ball. Many times they are already stretched out and the ball is thrown to the left, the right or high. Make sure they stretch to the ball.*

On a baseball thrown to the first baseman's right, he will step with his left foot to the outfield corner of first base and then stretch out with his right foot reaching with the left arm to receive the throw. (Sequence 4-2) If the throw is going to be a little farther off the bag, the first baseman can also put his right foot on the corner of the outfield side of first base and stretch out with his left foot giving him another 2 to 3 feet to receive the throw. (Sequence 4-3) This is on a ball that is going to be wide and a little bit farther off the target allowing the first baseman to have more range going toward his right.

On a ball thrown just off the infield side of the base, the first baseman will step on the infield side of the corner of the bag, stretch out and catch the ball just off the bag. (Sequence 4-4) If the ball is a little farther, notice in the next sequence how he is able to stretch out and catch the baseball on a 45-degree angle. (Sequence 4-5) This allows him to either catch the ball slightly off target or a ball that is going to be up the line where he has to reach out as far as he possibly can to catch it.

Sequence 4-2

Sequence 4-3

Sequence 4-4

Sequence 4-5

On a bang-bang play, the first baseman's ability and agility enable him to stretch as far as possible to catch the ball a step to a half-step quicker to make the play. It is imperative to have a first baseman who is able to stretch out, and has the flexibility and ability to make that play. (Photo 4-1)

Photo 4-1

Balls in the Dirt

One of the toughest plays for a first baseman is to catch a ball that is thrown in the dirt. There is going to be an area of 1 or 2 feet in front of the bag where he must decide to either scoop it on a short hop or give a little and try to catch it on the long hop. This is something that needs to be practiced over and over to allow the first baseman to become skilled in catching the ball in the dirt.

On a ball thrown right in front of the first baseman, he must stretch and catch the ball, scooping it forward by taking his glove and moving forward. This allows him to cut down on the hop of the ball. (Sequence 4-6) It also allows him to go forward with his hand and get the short hop. This is also used on the backhand play.

Sequence 4-6

Sequence 4-7

As you see in the next sequence, the first baseman scoops up the ball to his backhand by taking his hand and throwing forward. (Sequence 4-7) On long hops it is easy for the first baseman to stretch and the lower he gets the better view he gets of the baseball.

He can also reach out and catch the long hop if he gets the correct bounce which will allow him to catch the ball a little sooner. Any time you catch the ball deep, it is going to allow the runner another half-step before the ball hits the first baseman's mitt.

With runners in scoring position in a throw back to the infielder, especially with a runner on third, the first baseman must block a ball in the dirt. He cannot allow the ball to get by him. (Sequence 4-8) If it does, a run will score. In a bunt defense, if the ball is thrown in the dirt he must come off the bag and block it. This is very similar to a catcher not allowing the ball to get by him and go down the right-field line.

Sequence 4-8

Holding Runners

The first baseman wants to position himself with his right foot next to the bag, his left foot in fair territory with his shoulders open toward the pitcher ready to receive any type of throw. Just like the second baseman and shortstop, the first baseman must be ready for a wild throw, so he must expect a bad throw. When he receives a good throw he is ready to make the play.

His first priority is to catch the baseball and then apply the tag. When a ball is thrown in the dirt he must block it to keep the ball from going down the right-field line and the runner reaching second or third base.

In Sequence 4-9 the first baseman receives the ball and makes a quick tag on the runner going back into the base. A right-handed fielding first baseman will find he needs to go to his left knee as he makes the tag and rotate on his right foot to be able to reach in and tag a runner much quicker. (Photos 4-2 and 4-3)

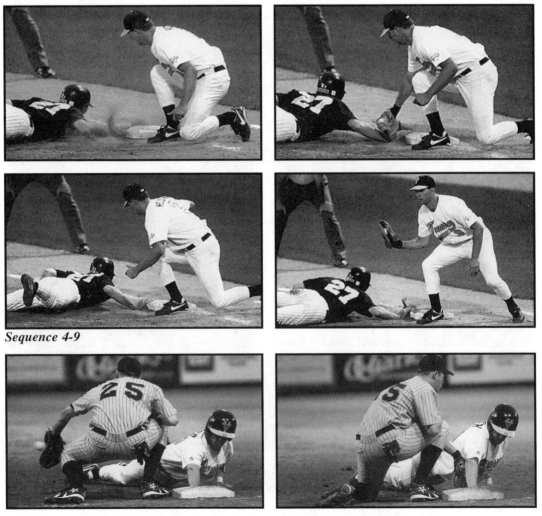

Sequence 4-9

Photo 4-2   *Photo 4-3*

On a pickoff throw, the first baseman wants to take the glove and go directly to the back corner of the bag. Popping the tag down and bringing the glove up makes for a quick tag.

Throwing to Second Base

With a runner on first base in a double-play situation, the first baseman is in a double-play depth. The right-handed first baseman, after catching the ball and starting to throw to second base, must rotate his shoulders and feet, and square up his shoulders which allows him to point his lead shoulder to second base when throwing to the outfield side of second and starting the double play. It is essential that he rotate his feet and get into position to make a good accurate throw to second. (Sequence 4-10)

Sequence 4-10

In the next sequence, the left handed first baseman has a much easier play as he fields the ball, shuffles his feet and throws to second base. (Sequence 4-11)

On pickoff throws from the pitcher, with a runner on first, the first baseman must square up his shoulders and come to the infield side of first base allowing him to make a good throw with the shortstop covering second base.

With a runner on third, it is imperative that the first baseman look the runner back before he throws to second base in a first and third situation. The key here is to go to the baseball, move toward the infield side of first base allowing him not to throw in the path of the runner as he throws the ball to the shortstop.

Sequence 4-11

Fielding Bunts and Slow Rollers

Probably one of the toughest plays for the first baseman is a bunted ball or a swinging bunt chopped down the first baseline between the pitcher and the first baseman.

Who covers first base and who goes after the ball? What is the communication? If the pitcher can make the play he must call off the first baseman by yelling "Ball! Ball!" which tells the first baseman to break back towards first and the pitcher will easily throw to first to get the out. If the pitcher cannot get the ball, he must yell, "Take it! Take it!" and continue to first base allowing the first baseman to field the ball and throw to the pitcher covering first base as in Sequence 4-12.

Sequence 4-12

Throws to the Pitcher Covering First

A common play finds the first baseman fielding a ground ball and throwing or giving an underhand flip to the pitcher covering first base.

On a ball hit to a first baseman the pitcher should always be breaking toward first and be ready to cover if the first baseman needs him. If the first baseman can get to first base, then he should call off the pitcher and let him know that he can make the play. If not, he should throw to the pitcher, leading him with a good accurate throw to complete the play and get the out.

If the first baseman is closer to the pitcher, he must give him a good underhand flip, getting the glove out of the way and allowing him to cover first base to get the out. (Sequence 4-13)

Notice how the first baseman takes the ball out of the glove, moves the glove away from his hand and with his bare hand gives a good flip with a stiff wrist. He follows his throw several steps to allow him to make a good, accurate, quick throw.

Sequence 4-13

This is a timing play and must be practiced over and over allowing the first baseman to know each pitcher and how well he moves, how agile he is and how quick he is.

It is important for the first baseman to lead the pitcher. This is a timing play. He wants to try to get the ball to the pitcher before the pitcher gets to the bag giving him a chance to catch the ball and then touch the base and be in a position to turn back to the infield ready for the next play.

Bunt Plays

The first baseman becomes extremely important on balls bunted down the first-base line with a runner on first. Most of the time he makes that play by picking the ball up and throwing to the second baseman covering first. The pitcher also is going to cover the area right in front of the plate and the first baseman has the first-base line.

If the ball is rolling, the first baseman must make sure to pick the ball up with both the bare hand and the glove, square his shoulders and be in position to throw back to first base.

If the first baseman can field the ball and tag the runner without throwing, then this, of course, is a much easier play. If the first baseman wants the baseball and the pitcher is converging on the ball at the same time, he must call him off by yelling, "Ball! Ball! Ball!" to allow the pitcher to get out of his way so he can field it cleanly and throw to first base.

If the pitcher calls, "Ball! Ball! Ball!" then the first baseman should move out to the right or go to his knees to allow the pitcher to make the play and have a clear throw to the second baseman covering first.

One of the plays a first baseman can make is a timing play between the pitcher and the first baseman. If the pitcher becomes set, there will be a counting system such as one-thousand-one, one-thousand-two and the pitcher will kick and go to the plate on the count of one-thousand-two with the first baseman breaking just before. This allows the first baseman to get in position to field the ball quicker, throwing the runner out at second base and getting the lead run.

It is essential that the pitcher kicks up right after the first baseman breaks in. If not, the runner will steal second base easily. To keep the runner honest, if you have this defensive play in your playbook, you must also put in the pick play. This is where the first baseman breaks in and then breaks back to first base and the pitcher kicks and throws to first base picking off the runner.

This is usually run after the first baseman has run the first play breaking in early and either the pitch was a ball or the runner has fouled it off or bunted through it. Now the defense will come back with the pick play at first base as in Sequence 4-14, allowing the first baseman to break back in and pick off the runner who is sleeping.

A great defensive first baseman can save his team a lot of runs in the course of a season. As I said earlier, the trend is away from the power-hitting first baseman and toward one who is a respectable hitter as well as a great defensive player.

Keep in mind that defense wins games and a great defensive first baseman can be a major asset in pursuit of that goal.

Sequence 4-14

5

Shortstop and Second Base

The double play is often called a pitcher's best friend.

A team that is strong up the middle will win a lot more ballgames than one that is just mediocre. Middle infielders can get a team out of a tough situation or give it new life with a snazzy double play.

It is important for the second baseman and shortstop to know each other thoroughly. They accomplish this with hours of practice working on feeds, pivots and throws to learn what each other does on certain plays.

The first rule to remember is get one out before you go for two. Catch the ball, pivot, throw the ball to first and then get out of the way of the runner. Breaking this sequence will lead to problems.

We always have our infielders get the lead runner first, then go for two if it is there to get. It doesn't help your team to get the lead runner and then throw wildly to first, allowing the runner to advance to second in scoring position. If you don't have a play, don't throw it. It takes two singles to score the runner from first.

When there is a runner on first and a double play in order, it is important that the middle infielders cheat in three or four steps toward the plate and one or two steps toward second base to be in position to get to the bag and be under control.

It is also important for the middle infielders to get to the bag in time to receive the throw. With a right-handed hitter, the second baseman will take the throw on a steal attempt. The shortstop will cover when a left-handed hitter is at bat. It is also important that the infielder let the pitcher know who is covering the bag.

Other important factors for the middle infielders to be aware of:

- Field conditions — slow, wet or fast.
- What pitch is being thrown.

Playing the hitter is extremely important. Even though you might be cheating in and over toward the bag in double-play depth, one or two steps in either direction can make a difference in completing the double play.

Getting to the base under control is of utmost importance. The only way that this can be done is to "cheat" toward the base, and once the ball is hit, break toward the base as quickly as possible. As the second baseman or shortstop gets within 5 feet of the base he should shorten his steps and get under control. His knees should be slightly bent and his hands up at chest level, relaxed and ready for any kind of a throw. If the middle infielder looks for a bad throw he will never be surprised when one comes.

He should line his body up with the direction of the throw from the other middle infielder and be about a foot behind the base ready to receive the throw.

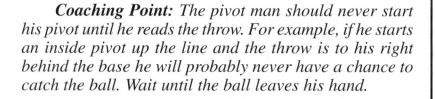

Coaching Point: *The pivot man should never start his pivot until he reads the throw. For example, if he starts an inside pivot up the line and the throw is to his right behind the base he will probably never have a chance to catch the ball. Wait until the ball leaves his hand.*

Feeds from the Shortstop

Every double play starts with a clean pick from the shortstop or second baseman and a quick throw to the pivot man covering the base. It is important for the shortstop to first catch the ball before he ever thinks about throwing the ball to the second baseman.

Too many times a middle infielder will start to look up toward the bag and take his eyes off the ball. This may cause him to bobble it, ending the chances for the double play or even getting one out.

Ball Hit Directly at the Shortstop

A shortstop's first task on a routine double play ball is to concentrate on receiving the ball. He should cheat a little bit on his position with his left side open to free his hips so that as he catches the ball he can easily rotate and throw the ball to the second baseman.

Notice in Sequence 5-1 that as he catches the ball he does not come up to throw the ball to second base; he just pivots, keeping his shoulders level, and turns and throws the ball to the second baseman.

Sequence 5-1

Also notice that when he throws three-quarters he keeps his wrist on top of the ball to get a good 12-6 rotation to the pivot man. There are times when he will have to throw sidearm. This is especially true on a ball hit to his right where he gets in front of it but his momentum is carrying him a little toward third base. He will drop down and throw the ball from the low three-quarters but still be able to make an accurate throw.

One of the keys here is that the infielder keep his feet planted and shift his weight to his right foot as he throws the ball to second base on the pivot. He does not want to readjust his feet on a ball hit right to him or on a ball hit four to five steps to his right.

Ball Hit to his Backhand

There are times when the shortstop will not have time to get in front of the ball and will have to make a backhand play to start the double play. Again, the key is to make sure to get the first out. Anytime the ball is hit to the backhand there is a chance that you are only going to be able get one out instead of two.

In Sequence 5-2, the player backhands the ball with his left foot extended forward as he receives the ball. He then crosses over with his right foot, plants, pushes off and makes a good chest-high throw to the second baseman to start the double play.

Sequence 5-2

Ball Hit to his Left

It is important for the shortstop to give a good accurate feed following his throw and make sure the second baseman is able to see the ball out of his glove.

Once the shortstop catches the ball, he wants to get his glove hand away from his body as he takes the ball out and prepares to flip it underhanded to the second baseman. This allows the pivot man, or second baseman, to see the ball and get a good view of it as it comes out of the shortstop's hand.

Notice in Sequence 5-3 how the shortstop follows his throw and gives a good throw with a stiff wrist allowing for consistency in the feed. You do not want a loop in the throw here; throw on a line to the second baseman.

Sequence 5-3

Slow-Hit Ground Ball

There are times when a shortstop is going to have to come in and make the throw on the run to start the double play. This is usually on a slowly hit ball that brings the shortstop up and in the baseline between second and third. It is important for him to come in and catch the ball on the run, making a controlled sidearm throw to the second baseman. If the shortstop does not come up to get the ball and catches it behind the baseline there is a good chance that he will get neither the runner at second or turn a double play.

By coming and getting the ball and starting the double play on the run, he will have an opportunity to get one for sure and many times two. This is a play that is only executed on a slowly hit ground ball where a shortstop has to come in and get it.

Sequence 5-4

Shortstop Pivots

The key to starting the double play is for the shortstop and middle infielder or second baseman to get to the bag under control. There are basically two pivots that a shortstop is going to make — outside of the bag or inside the bag. It really all depends on the throw from the second baseman.

Most of the time, the shortstop is going to take the outfield side or drag his right foot on the back corner of the base as he comes across the bag to start the double play. As you see in Sequence 5-4 he steps with his left foot to catch the ball and drags his right foot across the bag, then steps with his left foot to throw. Notice how he squares his shoulders to throw to first as he releases the ball.

In high school and college the runner must slide straight into the bag. By taking the inside or the back side of the bag or coming across the bag and positioning his body away from the base, it helps to avoid a collision with the runner sliding into second base. It also keeps the runner from breaking up a double play.

Inside Pivot

There are times when the second baseman will throw the ball into the infield side of second base forcing the shortstop to take the inside route to complete the double play. The shortstop will catch the ball and at the same time touch the inside corner of the base with his left foot. He then pushes off and steps to the right with his right foot while squaring up his shoulders and finishing by throwing to first base. (Sequence 5-5)

Sequence 5-5

This does two things:

1) It takes him out of the runner's path.

2) Quickens the throw to first base by using the inside track. This also is a pivot that is used on a throw from the pitcher which allows him to take the shortest distance between two points which is the inside track.

I have often seen the pitcher throw to the shortstop who takes the outside route to cover the bag. On a low throw the ball hits the bag and deflects to the left or right. Taking the inside track shortens the throw and also gives the shortstop an opportunity on a wild throw to position his body so that he at least gets one out by catching the ball and tagging second base.

Shortstop Unassisted

Whenever a middle infielder can catch the ball and complete the double play without having to make a throw to the pivot man, it allows the shortstop to call off the second baseman and complete the unassisted double play.

59

This play is particularly effective when the shortstop fields the ball going to his left as shown in Sequence 5-6. He is able to step on the bag with his left foot, and plant and throw using the bag as a protection from the incoming base runner. Also notice as he finishes his throw that he can hop into the air by pushing off with his left foot allowing him to keep the runner from sliding into his left foot.

Sequence 5-6

Second Base Pivots

If the throw is going to be low or in the dirt I want my pivot man to come across the base and catch the ball, thus eliminating the double play. If the throw is wide then he can go to either side attempting to hold one foot on the base for a force out. This technique can be used for several reasons:

- Last out of an inning.
- Ball in the hole.
- Bobbled ball close to the base.
- A slowly hit ball to the third baseman, which allows the pivot man only time to get the lead runner. The second baseman should come off the base after he makes the play to prevent being hit by the sliding runner.

It is important for a second baseman to learn more than just on pivot. This helps him to handle different kinds of throws. The throw will dictate what pivot he will use and will keep him from getting hurt. If he is always using the "straddle method" the runner will know where to slide to break up a double play. This will also depend on what level of baseball you are playing. There are rules in high school and college to protect the pivot man, but in professional ball the pivot man is "open season."

Left foot — inside

The pivot man assumes the ready position at the base. As he reads the throw he steps on the base with his left foot, catching the ball with two hands and pushing off the base planting with his right foot, then steps and throws to first base. (Sequence 5-7)

Sequence 5-7

Two very important points to remember:

1) When you push off the base, push off at a slight angle toward first to get momentum on your throw.

2) Open up your left foot and point it toward first base. If you leave it pointing toward third you could injure your knee if the runner slides into your leg.

When the pivot man becomes comfortable with this pivot, he can start to "cheat" a little. Instead of catching the ball and then stepping back, he can step back and catch the ball simultaneously to save some valuable time and become quicker.

Left foot — behind

This pivot uses the same technique as the left foot inside except that the second baseman touches the left-field side of the base and pushes off behind the base with his right foot, then steps and throws to first.

This pivot is used when there is a wide throw to the pivot man's right or a ball hit to the shortstop's left in the hole. (Sequence 5-8) This type of pivot protects the pivot man a little more because the runner has to slide over the base to get him.

Sequence 5-8

Left foot — across

This pivot is used when the ball is hit to the third baseman or to the right of the shortstop. It allows the second baseman to go get the ball and save valuable time. It also puts the pivot man a couple of feet in front (third base side) of the base, which makes it harder for the runner to break up the double play. In this sequence (5-9) the pivot man approaches the base under control. When he reads the throw he steps on the base with his left foot and crosses over with his right. As his right foot is about to hit the ground he should catch the ball with two hands, then step and throw to first.

If the third baseman could throw the ball a little to the second baseman's left, then he could go across in a slight angle toward first to get more on his throw instead of stepping directly toward third.

Sequence 5-9

Straddle

The straddle is a technique used by players who usually don't have real quick feet. This method allows them to position their feet on each side of the base, then catch the ball and throw. They never worry about touching the base and seldom do.

In this sequence (5-10) the pivot man approaches the base with his toes beside the corners of the base. As he catches the ball he has already shifted his weight to his right foot. Now all he has to do is throw the ball. This technique saves time and allows him to get rid of the ball faster. Notice that he stays over the base instead of going across or behind. This is done on a hard hit ball or when there is a slow runner at first and you don't have to worry about getting taken out.

Sequence 5-10

Remember, I said the throw dictates the pivot. Using the straddle method you can step behind, in front, or in back of the base and still throw to first. For example, if the throw is to the pivot man's right, he steps with his right foot to the left-field side of the base, dragging his left foot across the base, then throws to first.

Step – across (right foot)

This is a takeoff from the straddle method. This technique is used on slow rollers to shortstops near the base. We tell our shortstops to give the second baseman an underhanded feed to the first-base side of second. This allows the pivot man to "cheat" and get more momentum on his throw. I recommend this method only when the middle infielders have played together for a while and have spent hours in practice working on it.

In the next sequence(5-11), the pivot man steps across the base with his right foot while dragging his left foot. He catches the ball with two hands when his right foot hits the ground, then throws. This allows him to get rid of the ball more quickly.

Right Foot

This method is used when the ball is hit hard to the shortstop or third baseman and the pivot man doesn't get to the base in time. The second baseman might be playing a little farther from the base because of a left-handed batter. Remember, you still have to cover some ground in that situation. Also, on some ground balls hit hard

Sequence 5-11

to the third baseman he will come up throwing instead of taking a shuffle step to allow the pivot man to get to the base.

In this sequence (5-12) the second baseman gets the throw behind (right-field side) the base. He steps with his right foot on the base, then pushes off and throws to first base. Even though he is in the base line, he will still be able to hop over the runner. This pivot can also be used on a hard-hit ground ball with a slow runner at first.

Sequence 5-12

Avoiding Runners

The pivot man must know how to avoid the sliding runner. The best method is to hop over the runner by pushing off the left foot.

In Sequence 5-13 you see the pivot man hopping in the air off his left foot. This method allows him to avoid the runner and avoid being injured. Also notice the left foot pointing toward first base. This keeps the pivot man from injuring the knee in case the runner happens to take him out.

You see the runner getting there early and breaking up the double play. But, notice the pivot man hopping into the air to prevent a collision. If the pivot man knows how to avoid a runner he will be more comfortable in turning a double play.

Sequence 5-13

Throwing to First Base

The second baseman needs to be able to throw from all positions. If he gets a low feed he needs to throw from down there. If he gets a high throw needs to throw over the top or at three-quarters. The best throw is three-quarters, but sometimes you will have to throw sidearm. The throw should be quick and accurate.

These are several ways to turn the double play at second base. It is important to find out what method is best for your players and then have them spend hours perfecting it.

Feeds from the Second Baseman

The old cliche, *get one before you get two,* is so important. The two essentials I found in starting the double play are:

1) Field the ball cleanly.

2) Give a good feed to the pivot man, chest-high where he can easily start the double play.

Ground Ball Hit Directly at the Second Baseman

The second baseman should attempt to field the ball a little right of center by dropping his right foot back. This allows him to open up his hips and be in position to quickly and accurately start to feed toward the shortstop. The second baseman will open his hips by rocking backward onto his right foot, pivoting and throwing to the shortstop with his elbow up and his wrist on top of the ball putting a good 12-6 rotation on it.

Even by throwing three-quarters he can still keep his wrist up and behind the baseball. Notice in Sequence 5-14 that the second baseman does not put his left knee on the ground to complete the pivot. Some second basemen will find this beneficial to give them balance and keep them from coming up when completing the double play. I do not want our middle infielders to readjust their feet in order to throw their hips open. Notice how the second baseman drops his glove allowing the shortstop to pick the ball up as quickly as possible.

65

Sequence 5-14

Ground Ball Hit to the Second Baseman's Right

Balls hit 15 to 20 feet from the bag give the middle infielder the opportunity to shuffle and toss underhanded to the shortstop to start the double play. The second baseman shows the ball to the shortstop as quickly as possible by flipping the ball underhand with a stiff wrist. It is important for the second baseman to get the glove down and away from the flip so that the shortstop gets a good view of the ball.

The second baseman doesn't have to rise up to throw. He can remain in a crouched position, tossing the ball underhand and following his throw as seen in Sequence 5-15. Following the throw allows for a more accurate, consistent toss.

Sequence 5-15

A Slowly Hit Ball in the Baseline

On a slowly hit ball that the second baseman has to come and get, you will notice that he will catch the ball and shovel it to the shortstop using a backhanded toss with his fingers rotating inward and tossing the ball backward. Again, it is important to have a stiff wrist in attempting this shovel toss. (Sequence 5-16)

If the shortstop does not think that the second baseman has a chance at the runner at second he must yell "1-1-1" or "2-2-2" on a bang-bang play to let him know he has the opportunity to get the runner at second base. Again, this is a play on a slowly hit ball where the second baseman has to come up in the baseline or in front of the baseline.

Sequence 5-16

Balls Hit to the Extreme Left

In Sequence 5-17 the second baseman fields the ball as he moves toward his extreme left, plants on his right foot, reverse pivots and throws back to the shortstop to start the double play. If there is any doubt in his mind that he might not get the runner at second base, using this pivot he must then just throw to first to get an out. This is a pivot that must be practiced over and over and over for consistency and technique.

 ***Coaching Point:** If the player can get in front of the ball, then he must always do that.*

The double play is the pitcher's best friend. The key to success is for the shortstop and the second baseman to spend countless hours on perfecting the pivots and feeds which will allow them to consistently be able to turn a double play when it really counts.

Sequence 5-17

Tag Plays

How many times have you seen the catcher make a good accurate throw to second only to have the runner slide safely under the tag? It happens a lot, often because the middle infielder did not know the proper way to receive a throw at second base.

There are basically two methods at taking a throw at second base. One is by straddling the base and the other is taking the throw in front of the base. I find the straddle is the best technique at putting the middle infielder in a position to make a quick accurate tag.

We want the infielder to take the throw while straddling the bag and then drop his glove directly in front of the base, allowing the runner's foot to slide into it. We do not want the infielder to reach for the runner. Let the runner tag himself out.

In Photos 5-1and 5-2 notice how the infielder catches the ball and goes directly in front of the base to take the throw. In Photo 5-3, the infielder takes the throw in front of the bag and gives the baserunner the opportunity to go to the back part of the base and avoid a tag. This is why the straddle method is much better than taking a throw in front of the base.

Photo 5-1

Photo 5-2

Photo 5-3

6
Third Base

The third baseman has to have the reactions of a rattlesnake. He has to be quick on his feet because the ball gets to third much faster than it does to any other position. Third base is called the hot corner because of that quickness.

Although the third baseman doesn't necessarily have to be as quick as the shortstop, center fielder or even the second baseman, he must have the ability to react quickly to a line drive or a hard-hit ball to his backhand. He must be able to react quickly to a ball hit laterally and also be able to come in on a slowly hit ground ball or bunted ball down the third-base line.

I have found that it takes a certain amount of courage and mental toughness to become a great third baseman. Many times balls are hit right at them extremely hard which they just have to get in front of, knocking them down and positioning themselves in a way to be able to throw out the runner at first base.

Photo 6-1

For this reason, it is important for a third baseman to get a little lower in his ready position as opposed to a shortstop or second baseman. (Photo 6-1) The ball gets there so quickly that it is extremely important that his glove is a little closer to the ground than that of the others who have a little bit more time to react.

The third baseman must also be able to play in halfway or in a back position. He should know a little bit about the hitter, what type of hitter he is, whether he likes to bunt or swing away and try to hit the ball out of the ballpark. It is important that he knows how to play in, halfway back and be able to play off the line so that he can cover a little bit more ground to help his shortstop. So, he must be able to backhand the ball and move laterally which would help his shortstop cover more ground on the left side of the infield.

Slow Roller

The slow roller has to be the toughest play for a third baseman to make. The third baseman who can consistently make this play will solidify the left side of the infield. Whether it is a topped ball that trickles down the line or a slowly hit ball or even a bunted ball, the third baseman must be able to react quickly and come in and make that play.

There are basically two ways to make the slow roller play.

1) The one-handed play: The fielder comes in and reaches down and catches it with his glove hand and then brings it up and throws to the first baseman.

2) Two-handed play: This gives him a quicker release but doesn't allow him to throw the ball as hard as he would like to, whereas the one-handed play gives him the opportunity to catch the ball and allows him to throw a little bit harder but with a slower release.

The player's approach really depends on the angle of the ball. On a slowly hit ball to his left, he wants to approach the ball, catching the ball on the glove side, outside his foot and then throwing on the next step which allows him to take his momentum toward first base.

Sequence 6-1

Notice in Sequence 6-1 that instead of standing all the way up and releasing the ball, the infielder will throw him a low three-quarter or sometimes sidearm. The key here is to try to get the wrist in position to get good rotation on the baseball realizing that it is going to curve back in toward the first-base line at first base. Therefore he should set his sights on the inside of first base allowing the ball to run in toward the first baseman.

You would like for the player to be able to catch and throw on the next step but he is going to take an extra step using the one-handed method. It is true that he will have a little bit more on his throw but it is going to force him to take another step in the process which will cause the release to be a little bit slower.

The two-handed method allows the fielder to catch the ball off his left foot, reaching in with both hands and releasing the ball quickly. As the right foot plants he is able to get the throw off on the next step.

Notice in Sequence 6-2 that he catches the ball on the inside of the left foot which allows him to come in contact with the baseball with his bare hand a little quicker allowing him to release the ball with a good 3-9 rotation giving the first baseman a little bit better opportunity to receive the baseball. With the one-handed method you get more of a 12-6 rotation on the baseball which causes the ball to fade back in toward the first-base line.

Sequence 6-2

Using both methods the third baseman should come in and as he gets about 6 feet away from the baseball, shorten up his steps and get into position to field the ball. He wants to go hard until just about six steps and then put himself in a position to throw the baseball with control.

Also notice in the two-handed method going down the line that the infielder is fielding a ball that is more toward the third-base line to his right. Notice the angle that he takes as he takes two steps toward the line to get a better angle so that his momentum is going straight toward the catcher as opposed to going straight to the baseball where his momentum would take him toward foul territory at third base. He rounds off the ball and positions himself to throw the ball toward first base giving him an opportunity to free his hips a little better as he throws to first.

Sequence 6-3

Notice in Sequence 6-3 how the third baseman comes in and picks up a dead ball and throws to first base. This play is only used when the ball has stopped rolling. Never pick up a ball that is still rolling toward third. Notice the infielder here has rounded off the ball and is reaching down and picking up the ball inside his left foot allowing him to be able to throw off his right foot.

When the ball is rolling down the line, there are times when with an extremely quick runner that the only play is to come up and pick it up with a bare hand. This is a ball that has almost come to a stop and is barely trickling down the line. If the ball happens to be bouncing down the line, he needs to pick it up using one of the two methods (one hand/two hand glove method).

Backhanded Slow Roller

There are two ways to play a slow roller that is hugging the left-field line with an infielder playing off to his extreme left. One is to come up and backhand it, getting a little bit more on your throw; the other is to use the slow roller method of coming in and receiving the ball and throwing on the run. Sometimes this gives you a quicker release but doesn't give you much on the throw. Here we want the player to go in a straight line to the point of the ball, backhand it and then crow-hop or shuffle step, getting the throw off by throwing with maximum effort and getting a good throw squarely to the first baseman. (Sequence 6-4) This allows the third baseman to get a quick release with a strong, accurate overhand throw to the first baseman.

Backhand Play

There have been great backhand plays over the years made by third baseman such as Brooks Robinson and Greg Nettles that really turned a World Series around. The backhand play enables the third baseman to play a little farther off the line and allows him to cover more ground. It all depends on how hard the ball is hit and the momentum that the third baseman has when he catches the ball.

In Sequence 6-5 you notice the third baseman receives the ball with his left foot planted and then crow-hops or shuffle steps back and completes the throw to the first baseman. This is a ball that is hit where his momentum gets him to the ball and is not

Sequence 6-4

necessarily a hard-hit ball down the line. He is able to backhand and then be in position to rotate back on his right foot, crow-hop and throw back to first base.

It is important that the third baseman here keep his nose behind the glove, open up and try to catch the ball in the webbing as opposed to catching it in the palm of the hand. If the ball hits the palm of the hand, most of the time it will have the tendency to pop out. Again, this is usually a slowly hit ground ball to his backhand that he is able to get to and shuffle step and throw back to first base.

Sequence 6-5

Sequence 6-6

On the ball that is hard hit down the line, you will notice in Sequence 6-6 that he catches the ball and his momentum takes him one step farther. In this case he must plant his right foot and be able to throw back to first base. As the third baseman takes the long step with his right foot, it gives him a strong base to push off of and throw back to first base. Notice as he catches the ball off his left foot he takes a long step to give him balance and a base to throw from. The throws from the backhand should be over the top which give good 12-6 rotation back to the first baseman.

Bunting Situations

This may be the most difficult play for a third baseman because he must know when to come in and get the ball and when to break back to third base to receive a throw from the pitcher on a force play. There are several things he must consider:

1) The quickness of his pitcher.

2) The speed of the runner at second base.

3) He must be able to read the ball off the bat quickly to see if it is a hard bunted ball or a ball that is bunted softly that the pitcher or catcher will be able to field.

Photo 6-2 illustrates how the third baseman positions himself so that he can see the runner, the pitcher and the hitter.

> ***Coaching Point:*** *It is extremely important that the defense gets an out. If the third baseman makes the mistake, he must make the mistake by coming in and getting a ball that possibly could have been thrown to third base, calling off the pitcher and getting an out at first base. We cannot afford to blow this play and allow the other team to load the bases with no outs.*

If the ball is bunted extremely hard, the third baseman must come in and field the ball and throw the runner out at first base. Remember, it is the bunter's job to bunt the ball by the pitcher hard enough that the third baseman must come in and throw him out at first base. So let's try to take advantage of what they are giving us. Get an out in this situation.

If the pitcher is able to field the ball cleanly and cut the angle off, his first priority is to throw the ball back to the third baseman to try to get a force out. If the third baseman reads this, he must break back to the bag and get into a position to field the ball just like a first baseman getting the force out on the throw coming from second base.

If the third baseman happens to break in and the pitcher fields the ball he must yell "1-1-1" so that the pitcher sets his feet and throws to first as opposed to setting his feet for a throw to third base with no third baseman there.

Again, if we blow this play, it is important that the defense still get an out. In this situation the third baseman must run in yelling "1-1-1" so that the pitcher knows that the third baseman is not at third base.

Photo 6-2

This takes a lot of work, but through coaching drills and bunting situations at practice, a third baseman will get to know the quickness of his pitchers and learn to recognize which balls he must charge and throw out the runner, and when to break back to third to receive a throw from the pitcher.

Double Play Balls

In starting the double play it is important that the third baseman realize we must get one before we get two. Catching the ball cleanly and then giving an accurate throw to the second baseman is extremely important. He wants to try to throw the ball letter high on the inside part of second base so that the second baseman can catch the ball and keep his momentum going toward first base on the throw.

Sequence 6-7

If the ball is hit directly to the third baseman, we want him to catch the ball and then try to throw the ball over hand or three-quarters which gives good rotation on the throw to the second baseman.

In Sequence 6-7 the third baseman has caught a ball hit right at him and starts the double play with a good, accurate throw to the second baseman. On balls hit to the left that he has to be moving for, a third baseman may throw from a low position as in Sequence 6-8. This gives him the ability to release the ball a little quicker as opposed to standing up and then throwing the ball. This takes more practice but gives the third baseman a quicker release.

Sequence 6-8

Becoming a great third baseman takes a tremendous amount of work, courage and quickness to be able to make all the different plays during the course of a season.

7
Outfield Play

A good defensive outfielder needs good speed and the ability to get a good jump on the ball. Outfielders are the last line of defense. From that statement alone you can see that they are very important to a team.

Today, however, it is difficult to find outfielders at any level who can both field and throw the baseball consistently. Many have great arms but don't know the proper fundamentals of catching and throwing. Other outfielders may have average arms but field and release the ball quickly and accurately.

Ball Hit Directly at the Outfielder

Assume a ball is hit so that an outfielder has to move very little. The ball has been hit directly to the right fielder, for example. There's a man on third base, and he will be going on the catch. What is the proper technique necessary to catch the ball and throw the man out at the plate?

The first thing is to establish momentum toward the plate. Never catch the ball with dead feet. In Sequence 7-1 the outfielder approaches the ball by stepping first with his left foot, then his right as he catches the ball (with two hands) a little left of center. Catching the ball a little left of center is more natural for the athlete, and as he crow-hops it gives his arm time to get the full swing that he needs.

Catching the ball on the throwing side is unnatural and will cause the outfielder to short-arm the ball like an infielder. Notice in Sequence 7-1 that the outfielder has caught the ball a little left of center and it has not caused him to take any additional steps.

As he catches the ball, the outfielder should crow-hop and bring the right foot forward in front of the left foot. He wants to throw on this step. So many times you will see an outfielder who is out of control take additional unnecessary steps.

As he takes the ball out of the glove, he wants to try to grip the ball across the four seam. This enables the outfielder to get better rotation on the ball. Ideally you would like to have a 12-6 rotation on the ball. This keeps the ball from trailing to the

Sequence 7-1

right side. Also notice in Sequence 7-1 how the outfielder gets his body turned so that the shoulder is pointing toward home plate. Your shoulder is like the sight on a gun — where you point it is where the ball is going to go.

In Sequence 7-1 the outfielder has, 1) pointed his shoulder, and 2) turned his right foot parallel with his left foot so he can drive forward and has raised his left leg like a pitcher to get momentum to the plate. As he throws the ball, he will get his body behind it. Outfielders often throw with just their arm. Also notice the glove position. Throwing the glove out to the side throws the shoulder off target. The glove should just come down past the left knee.

Remember, an outfielder throwing to a base should always throw through the cutoff man. This keeps the hitter from advancing to the next base.

Sequence 7-2

78

Rounding a Fly Ball

In certain throwing situations an outfielder will have to round the baseball off in order to get into a position to allow his body to get into the throw. In Sequence 7-2, the right fielder is rounding the baseball off to get his body into the throw to third base. He wants to pivot on his right foot and use a crossover step to allow him to get the quick start. As the outfielder gets closer to the baseball, he shortens his steps a little allowing him to get under control. He wants to catch the ball above his head with his left foot forward.

> ***Coaching point:*** *If the outfielder doesn't shorten his steps a little, he will not be able to throw on the next step. Longer strides will cause him to take more steps. After he catches the ball he uses the crow-hop (right foot over and in front of left) to throw the baseball. The outfielder wants to get a little height to his crow-hop to allow the arm to complete the full swing. He also has a nice follow-through which is the natural reaction on a good throw.*

Fly Ball Hit Over Outfielder's Head

A ball that is hit over the outfielder's head calls for a "drop step." If the ball is hit over his left shoulder, then he will drop step with his left foot and use a crossover step with his right foot. If the ball is hit over his right shoulder, he will drop step with his right foot and use a crossover with his left (Sequence 7-3).

Sequence 7-3

An outfielder should never drift on a fly ball. If an outfielder can drop step and go back and then come back into the ball, he has been very successful on the catch. This enables the outfielder to get his momentum going to the plate. If he doesn't, he has to throw the ball without momentum limiting the distance the ball will travel. In Sequence 7-3, the outfielder does a fine job of coming back into the ball. Notice how he catches the ball with two hands just a little left of center.

Reverse Pivots

On a ball hit over the outfielder's head where he must drop step and break straight back it is important that he stay in a straight line as he breaks back to receive the ball. There are basically three techniques to use on balls hit hard over his head:

1) He has to break back with his eyes fixed on the ball.

2) He will break back and take quick glances at the ball.

3) The ball is hit way over his head forcing him to break back at a dead run, taking his eye off the ball and then turning and finding the baseball. This is the ball that is hit 20 to 30 yards or more over his head.

In Sequence 7-4 the outfielder breaks for the ball in a straight line, reaches up and is able to make the catch. The key here is not to slow down, and to contain a run at full speed and not drift on the baseball.

Sequence 7-4

In the next sequence (7-5) the outfielder has turned the wrong way. This often happens because of wind or poor judgment. To make a wrong into a right, the outfielder must reverse pivot, remain in a straight line, make the adjustment and catch the ball in full stride without slowing down. Things to think about here:

1) Remain in a straight line as you reverse pivot.

2) Do not look down at the ground.

3) Reverse pivot as quickly as possible. Rotate your head and pick up the baseball as quickly as you can.

80

Sequence 7-5

Many times on a reverse pivot it is necessary to move left or right to go get the baseball. Sometimes the wind will blow the ball. For example, the right fielder may open up on his throwing side but the ball drifts toward the line and he must reverse pivot to get to the ball. This often happens when a right-handed hitter hits to right field. The ball tends to hook toward the line. Some outfielders open up to the right side, then have to reverse pivot and get the baseball. This a great technique to learn.

Catching The "Do-or-Die" Ground Ball

There are three general rules to remember on ground balls:

1) On balls hit sharply and directly at the fielder, throw out the lead runner.

2) On balls that force the fielder to run toward the play, look at the lead runner. There is plenty of time to readjust and throw to second base.

3) On balls hit to the left or right and the fielder is moving away from the infield, throw to second base.

See where the runner is in relation to the base when getting control of the ball. If he has rounded third, throw to second or third. If he has just touched third when the fielder is in position to throw, he has a good chance to throw him out at home.

Sequence 7-6

The "do-or-die" play is usually a game-saving throw. The outfielder should charge the ball on his first few steps as hard as he can. As he approaches the ball, he shortens his steps and almost comes to a complete stop. It is imperative that he sink in his knees and watch the ball into his glove. This keeps him under control (Sequence 7-6). He needs to catch the ball on the outside of his left foot.

> ***Coaching point:*** *It is important for the outfielder to catch the ball just off to the side of his left foot, as close as possible. (Photo 7-1) This will be a little quicker. (Then on the next step he wants to crow-hop and get in position to throw.) If the outfielder charges the ball too hard and doesn't use jab steps, then he will have to take extra steps to throw to the plate. For every one step the outfielder takes, the runner is taking two.*

Photo 7-1

Ball Hit to the Left or Right

The ball that is not hit hard to either side allows the outfielder to take a 45-degree angle up and round the ball off to cut down the distance. (Sequence 7-7) It is essential to charge hard until the last few steps where he will take a few jab steps. This gets him under control and able to throw on the next step. Charging too hard will cause him to rush his throw, which may cause it to be wild.

Take note in Sequence 7-6 how the outfielder has watched the ball all the way into the glove. A common fault is to look up at the runner before catching the ball. This usually results in a misplayed ball. The "do-or-die" is just what it means — "do-or-die," so it is imperative to watch the ball into the glove. Good outfielders make a tremendous contribution to a team, but they often go unnoticed until they have to make a "do-or-die" play.

Sequence 7-7

Playing the Fence

Coaches spend very little time preparing outfielders to play the fence. Any player can master this simple technique if he spends time with his coach on a series of drills.

It is important for each outfielder to know how far he is from the outfield warning track and the fence.

- How big is the outfield?
- How wide is the warning track?
- Once the outfielder hits the track, how many steps until he reaches the wall?
- What type of fence does he have — brick, metal, hurricane, chain-link?
- Does the ball bounce off of it or hit and drop?
- Are there poles exposed?
- Is he able to climb the fence?
- How tall is the fence?
- Can he get back and get up and over the fence?

These are the questions that every outfielder must answer before the game starts. Therefore, it is extremely important for the outfielder to know not only his own playing surface and outfield fence, but also the opponent's.

Baseball at the Base of the Wall

As the outfielder approaches the ball, he should put his throwing side closer to the fence. This puts him in a position to quickly throw the ball back to the infield.

On a ball lying dead near the wall or the fence, there are two basic approaches to retrieving the ball and throwing it back into the infield. On a ball that is right next to the fence, the player will have to go up and plant his body next to the ball, taking the baseball and pushing down, making sure he picks it up. We use the term "drive the ball into the ground." As he pushes down on the ball he makes sure he gets a good firm grip and shuffles his feet and throws back into the infield.

Notice in the next series (Sequence 7-8) on a ball that is right against the fence that kicks off, the outfielder must step over the ball, centering the ball in the midline of his body as he bends forward to pick it up. If the outfielder reaches down to pick it up without centering his body over the ball and just picks it up near his rear foot, he will have a tendency to pull away from the ball too soon, peek up to look at the runner and sometimes fail to pick the ball up cleanly. The outfielder's job is to get the ball back to the middle infielder as quickly as possible.

Remember that one good throw leads to another so it is important, as you can see in the sequence, that the outfielder gets the ball back to the infield using a shuffle step method as opposed to using a crow-hop. The shuffle step method gets the ball to the relay man more quickly and accurately.

Sequence 7-8

Playing the Wall or Fence

There are times when the fielder and the ball arrive at the fence at the same time. The only way to make this play is by knowing the number of steps to take from the warning track to the fence. The outfielder needs to realize how close he is to the wall as he approaches it. That is why it is important in pregame to determine if it takes three or four steps to reach the wall once he hits the track.

To get into position to make a catch off the wall, the outfielder should use his throwing hand to help brace the impact and also allow him to know when he has reached the wall. (Sequence 7-9) The outfielder wants to jump vertically after he reaches the wall which allows him to reach the highest point of his jump. Reaching out with his throwing hand can allow him to move up the fence and reach out to make that great catch.

If playing on a field with a chain-link fence the outfielder can use his cleats to reach in, hit the fence, and pull himself forward and up in order to cover more area above the fence, possibly robbing the hitter of a home run. Going to the glove side will cause the outfielder some problems because he cannot use his glove to reach out and touch the fence.

Sequence 7-9

I have found the key to playing the fence is a lot of drill work. Coaches should either hit fungoes or throw the ball to players working on going back on the fence and learning how to reach up and catch the ball off the wall.

There are times when balls will get over an outfielder's head and he is not going to have the opportunity to make the play. Therefore, it is important for him to pull up short to get in position to catch a ball coming off the wall, be in a throwing position ready to shuffle his feet and throw the ball back to the infield. Notice in the next sequence (7-10) that the outfielder has rounded the ball off and is in position to catch the ball and throw it back into the infield. This is a ball that was hit over his head.

Sequence 7-10

As he approaches the wall he realizes that he is not going to be able to get to it, so he stops short of the wall and puts himself in position to catch the ball and throw back to the infield.

On a ball hit in a gap with a left fielder and center fielder converging, one player needs to go after the ball against the wall and the other player needs to break back off the wall in position to make the play if the other fielder doesn't get to the ball.

Play in the Sun

There is never an excuse for an outfielder to lose the ball in the sun. One of the pregame rituals should be to check the sun to see how it is going to be at game time.

Playing the sun

Do you need sunglasses? We have been in games from time to time where a player has lost the ball in the sun. We have all seen it. You look out and notice that he is not wearing sunglasses.

A flip-down model is available from Easton and a continuous wear model from Oakley. An outfielder can also use his glove to shield the sun. I think all three are very good. You should use your glove and some type of sunglasses to aid in blocking the sun.

This is something that is determined in pregame or during an inning. If the sun comes out from behind a cloud you should call time-out and go in and get a pair of sunglasses. The baseball sunglasses are worn under the visor of the cap and can be flipped out over the eyes.

The next step is to go to the outfield on sunny days with your glasses and your glove. Have the coach hit fly balls into the sun and work on catching balls using the flip-down or continuous wear glasses.

Dive Plays

When was the last time you saw an outfielder make a sensational diving play to end an inning or prevent a rally? This is one of the most exciting plays in baseball.

It really starts in practice. I have found that it is important to put your player in a game-like situation. At Tennessee we spend a lot of time with the outfielders on making diving catches because there are so many times during a season where a player has to dive for the ball or pull up short to keep it in front of him.

We tell our outfielders not to dive unless they are going to catch it. We don't want them to try to make a shoestring catch unless they have the opportunity to catch the ball.

Outfielders often dive for balls they really have no chance of catching. The ball gets by and the next thing you know the hitter is standing on third base with a triple. Or an outfielder dives for a ball when the score is 5-1 with runners on first and second and it turns into a 5-3 ballgame.

Therefore, you do not want to dive for a ball which, if missed, would give the opponents the opportunity to get back in the game, or a ball that, if missed in a close game with runners in scoring position, would result in a loss. The bottom line is: If you are going to dive for the ball, catch it.

It is important for the player to learn the proper technique in extending his body with his arm stretched out, glove open and ready to catch a ball in front with the proper technique. Notice after he catches the ball in Sequence 7-11 that he slides on his chest with his arms extended. Part of the injuries on dive plays occur when the arms roll up under the body.

Here the outfielder is able to work on forehand and backhand dives or dives directly in front of him where he has to come in at full speed, reach out and catch the ball, sliding in across the outfield just as he would slide into second base — which is very natural. I have found that the more they do this drill the more confident they get on the dive play, and this directly transfers into great dive plays during the season for the team.

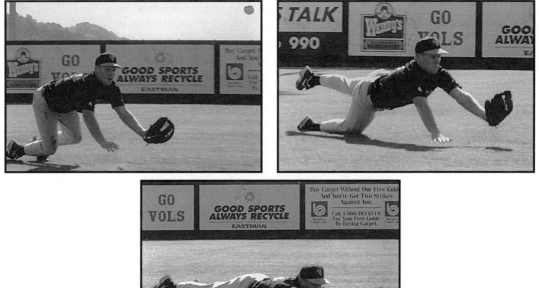

Sequence 7-11

Communication

The center fielder is the captain in the outfield. Team work is essential among all outfielders. On fly balls, the center fielder has priority over the other two outfielders. When coming in to catch a fly ball, it is essential that the outfielders yell, "I've got it, I've got it, I've got it" three times to allow the other outfielders to know that he is calling them off the ball.

Communication should be constant in the outfield. They should always be talking about the wind, the sun, the wet grass, throwing situations and balls hit into the gaps. The outside outfielder can help the other outfielder as to where to throw the baseball. Or if he bobbles the ball remind him to throw the ball into second base.

It is extremely important that they communicate on how they are playing hitters. Again, the center fielder is the captain and in charge of setting the defense as to whether they are playing 7½, 8 or 8½.

Backing Up Bases

The outfielder should be reminded that there is always a play to be made on backing up a base. Outfielders should never be standing in the outfield while a play is going on in the infield. They should be backing up some base, anticipating a bad throw from an infielder that could get in the outfield. Always look for a place to go, whether you are a right fielder backing up second, or wherever. Get at an angle and anticipate a wild throw.

The one time you do not back up a base would be the one time that there is an overthrow which could be a costly error. On pickoff plays such as one back to second base, make sure that the center fielder is rushing in as soon as he sees the pitcher turn to throw. This will allow him to be in a position on a wild throw to keep the runner from advancing to third. If he is not hustling in on a wild throw, the runner can easily get into third base. This is a perfect example of what we are talking about — anticipating a bad throw and being in a position to keep the runner from advancing to the next base.

Remember, the outfielders are the last line of defense.

8
Team Defense

In today's game, defensive alignment has become extremely important in restricting the productivity of the offense. If you go to the ballpark you will notice that the infield and outfield are moving on every hitter. In fact, some teams have the defense moving on each pitch. Others will have them moving when the hitter is behind in the count or ahead in the count. It is easy to see that baseball is not a game of simplicity.

Defensive Alignment

Before you start to move the defense you must have an idea where the hitter is going to hit the baseball. This information comes from closely examining the hitter to see where his weaknesses are:

- Where does he like the ball?
- What kind of hitter is he?
- Where does he usually hit the baseball?

A player who stands close to the plate usually will pull the ball whereas a player who stands away from the plate has a tendency to hit the ball the opposite way.

If we are seeing a player for the first time we will usually play him straight-up (8). There is some criteria involved that will determine where we play some players even if we have not seen them play. For example, if a left-handed hitter is facing a right-handed pitcher you will probably play a little toward the pull side (8½). It would be the opposite for a left-handed pitcher vs. a right-handed hitter. We would now shade him toward left field (7½) which is a slight pull to left.

You have to also consider where the player is hitting in the lineup. If he is hitting in the 1 or 2 spot he will probably spray the ball. The third, fourth, fifth and sixth hitters have a tendency to pull the ball while the seventh, eighth and ninth hitters are more likely to be late with their swings.

It is important for the infield and outfield to move together. Playing the infield straight-up and the outfield pulled leaves gaps in the defense. It is just like having a few keys off in a piano. We use a system here that makes it simple for our defense to move very quickly to an area that we want covered. The number system is 7, 7½, 8, 8½ and 9.

In diagram 8-1 the defense is playing an extreme pull to the left side. They are giving up the right side of the diamond. Notice how the shortstop and second baseman are playing a little deeper than normal. This helps them cover more ground laterally. The first baseman is pulled over toward second but needs to remain close enough to first to cover on a ground ball hit to the left side. The outfielders are instructed to look into the dugout to see what sign I am giving for each hitter. In photo 8-1 I am holding up my left arm which is the sign for 7.

In photo 8-2 you see the sign for 7½. This is a slight pull to left field. We use this alignment when we have a left-handed pitcher vs. a right-handed hitter. It can also be used when we feel that a hitter is a pull hitter but still hits the ball to right-center field. In diagram 8-2 the right fielder has taken away the gap in right-center.

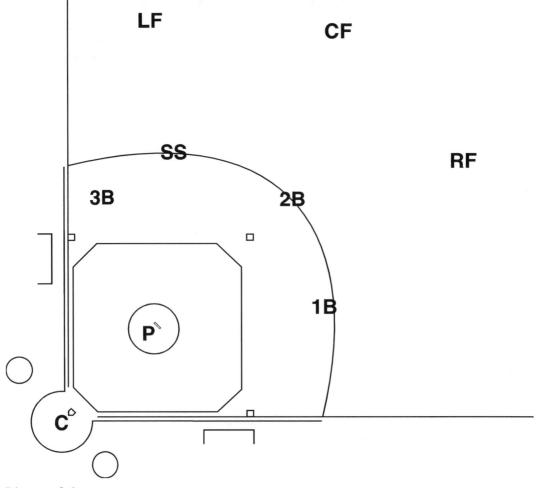

Diagram 8-1

Photo 8-1

Photo 8-2

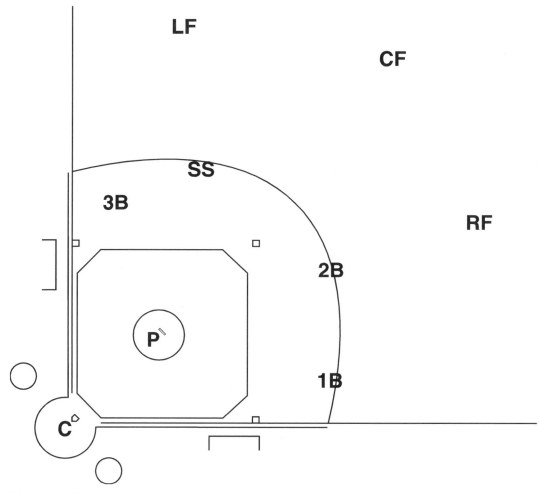
Diagram 8-2

Diagram 8-3 is how we play hitters when we aren't quite sure where they hit the ball. This is called straight away and photo 8-3 shows the sign for alignment 8.

Let's say, for example, that we have a right-handed pitcher vs. a left-handed hitter. We now would play an 8½ (diagram 8-4) which is a straight pull to the right side. Photo 8-4 shows the sign for 8½ which is given before the player is ready to hit. The defense moves into position and is ready for the pitcher to pitch.

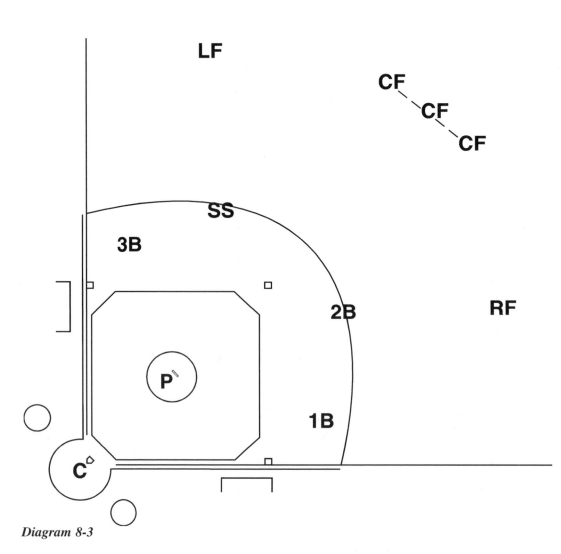

Diagram 8-3

Photo 8-3

Photo 8-4

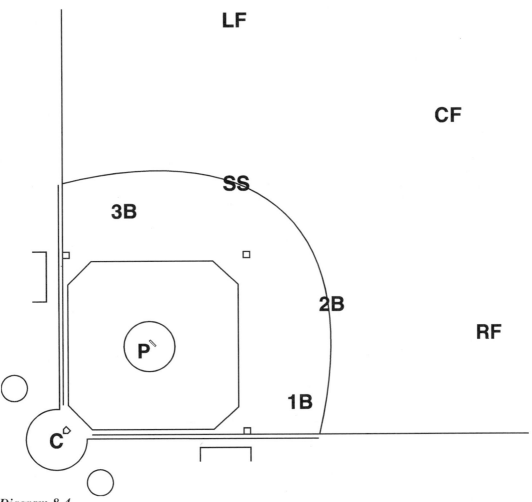

Diagram 8-4

If we have an extreme pull hitter to right we use defense alignment 9 (diagram 8-5). Photo 8-5 shows the sign for 9 which is just holding up the right arm. Again take note that the shortstop and second baseman are a little deeper to allow for more lateral coverage. The third baseman is also pulled off the line to cover more ground to his left.

The last defense alignment is called a bunch (diagram 8-6). In photo 8-6 I am holding up both arms together for the bunch sign. This alignment is used for a hitter who seldom hits the ball down the lines. He is known more as a "gap hitter" so the defense plays him more up the middle, giving him the lines.

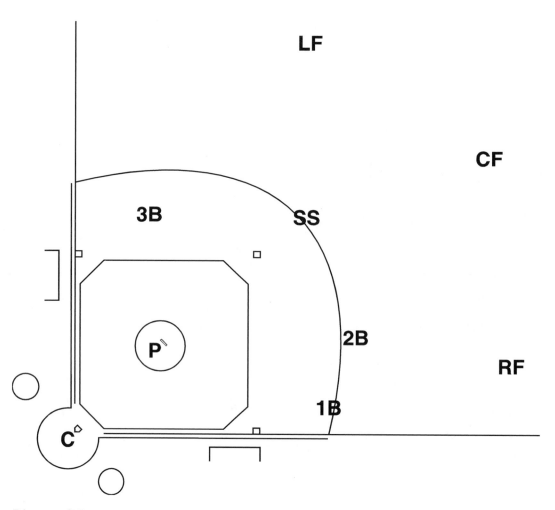

Diagram 8-5

Photo 8-5

Photo 8-6

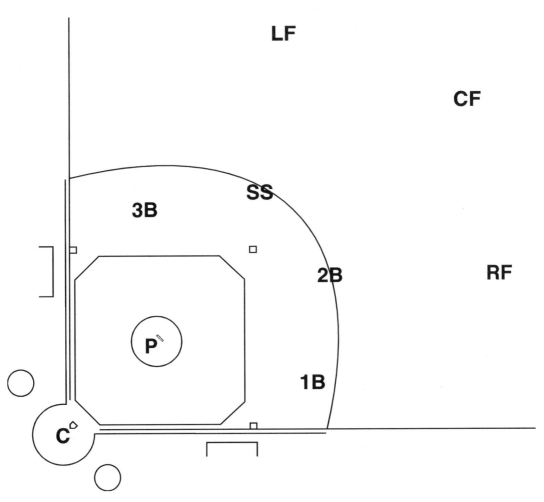

Diagram 8-6

After the defense gets the signs down, it's time to make some adjustments. The outfielders will line up in their alignment but must take into consideration which hand their glove is on. If the center fielder is right-handed and playing an 8, he will line up a few steps to his right. With his glove on his left hand he can afford to play a few steps to his right because of the easier catch going toward his left. The outfielders that play in left and right field with the glove on the hand closest to the lines can afford to play a couple of steps toward the gaps.

For a right-handed hitter, the right fielder can play a little shallower than normal. This is also true for the left fielder against a left-handed hitter. The outfielders would move into a 1 depth. This is four steps shallower than normal depth. The only exception would be a power hitter who hits the ball well to the opposite field. Then the off-side outfielder would play a normal depth.

We have a number system for the different depths. To have a player play in we use the number 1 as the sign. Number 2 would be a normal depth and 3 would be four steps back from a normal depth. An example of the 3 depth would be two outs and you don't want the ball hit over your head for extra bases. The outfielders would play a 3 to keep the hitter to just a single.

I mentioned earlier that some coaches like to move on the count whereas others prefer only to move on each hitter. When the hitter is ahead in the count 1-0, 2-0, 2-1 or 3-1, he is more likely to pull the ball. The outfielders should move four steps over and four steps back on each pitch. If the pitcher is ahead in the count 0-1, 1-2 or 0-2, the hitter is more likely to hit the ball up the middle or to the opposite field. Therefore, the outfielders would move four steps in and four steps over. The only exception would be for a hitter with extreme power. You would not want to move in four steps on each pitch. It would be better to move over just four steps. The key is for each outfielder to move on the count. If one outfielder doesn't move it creates a gap.

Bunt Defense

It has been said over and over that bunting is a lost art. If you tune into your Saturday morning highlight goof-up film, you will notice that there are a few plays defending the bunt.

It's often the little things in baseball that allow you to win games. The philosophy of today's game is pitching and defense. The team that has the best pitching and defense will win more than its share of games over the team known for its hitting. In the end, good pitching and defense will overcome good hitting. With this in mind, the key is to develop a strong defensive unit that will minimize mistakes.

Bunt Defense with Runner on First

With a runner on first base, the idea is to try to get the lead runner out at second base. The defense needs to be aware that we *must* get an out. If we don't get the lead runner, then we will settle on getting the hitter at first base. So many times teams try to force the situation, throw to second base and the runner ends up safe or advances on a wild throw.

Diagram 8-7 shows the movement of the right side of the infield. The first baseman must cover first base and then break toward home when the pitcher throws to the plate. If the first baseman leaves early, this allows the runner to steal second base. Remember, we are trying to get the lead runner. The second baseman comes in two steps then breaks directly toward first base. The reason for the movement toward the play (straight in) is in case the hitter fakes a bunt and then swings away. The right fielder breaks to back up first base after the ball has been bunted in case of a wild throw.

The pitcher, first baseman and third baseman come in to cover all areas where the ball could be bunted. If the third baseman does not field the ball, he must get back to cover third base or the lead runner will round second and head for third. It is the catcher's responsibility to get the third baseman to cover third.

The shortstop covers second base to take the throw if we have a play there. The center fielder will back the play up in case of a wild throw. If one occurs, it is the center fielder's job to keep the runner from advancing to third.

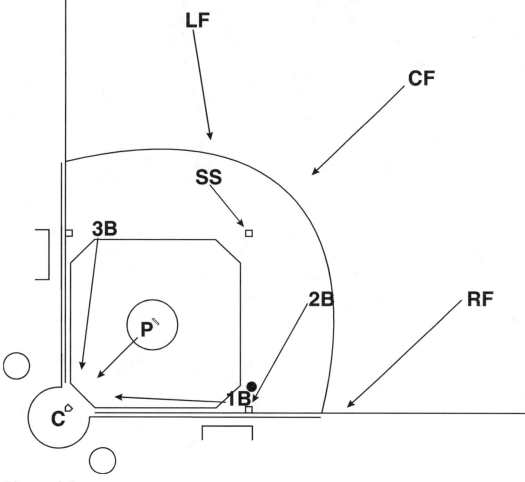

Diagram 8-7

Sequence 8-1

>
> ***Coaching Point:*** *Teach your outfielders to expect a bad throw. This way they will also be in a good backup position.*

There are two schools of communication here with this defense. One is to allow the catcher to read the play and yell to the infielders "Second," or "First". He decides where the ball is going to be thrown. If the catcher makes a mistake and the pitcher comes up, throws to second and the runner is safe, we are in trouble.

The other method is to allow the pitcher, first baseman and third baseman to read the bunt and decide where the throw should go. With constant practice, infielders can read the play and decide the proper throw. If a bunter makes a good bunt, we must get an out and throw to first. We have a saying: "When in doubt, get an out!" If an infielder bobbles the ball and was going to attempt a throw to second, he must get the out by throwing to first base.

In Sequence 8-1 we have a pickoff play to get the runner at first base. The first baseman takes three quick steps ... left, right, and then left toward the plate. The idea is to get the runner to relax and maybe lean or take a step toward second. Then the first baseman breaks back to the bag without taking his eyes off the pitcher. The pitcher kicks and throws to first, picking the runner off. This is a timing play that may or may not work. If the play doesn't work, no big deal, it simply sets up our next play. As I mentioned earlier, if the first baseman breaks early, then the runner can steal second or get a great jump which keeps the defense from throwing him out.

The next play will allow the first baseman to be able to leave early and get in good position to field the bunt and throw out the lead runner. Remember, the bunter is trying to bunt the ball to first because the first baseman is holding the runner on. In the meantime, the third baseman is camped out, hoping the bunter makes a mistake and bunts the ball to the third base side.

In Sequence 8-1 you will notice that it is a timing play. The first baseman breaks as the pitcher's hands come down just before he kicks his leg up. This allows the first baseman to get into a great position to get the lead runner. Keith Hernandez used this play effectively during the years he played professional baseball.

Bunt Defense with Runners on First and Second

Remember, the first rule is to get an out, but we are also trying to get the lead runner. The shortstop is the key man in this defense. He must hold the runner at second base close to the bag. The key is for the shortstop to yell back and then the pitcher will kick and throw to the plate. If the runner gets too much, then the pitcher will turn and throw to the second baseman for a pickoff.

This is the toughest play for a third baseman to make. The pitcher is supposed to cover the third base line. The third baseman is supposed to field the ball only if the pitcher cannot get to it.

Two things dictate the third baseman making the play:

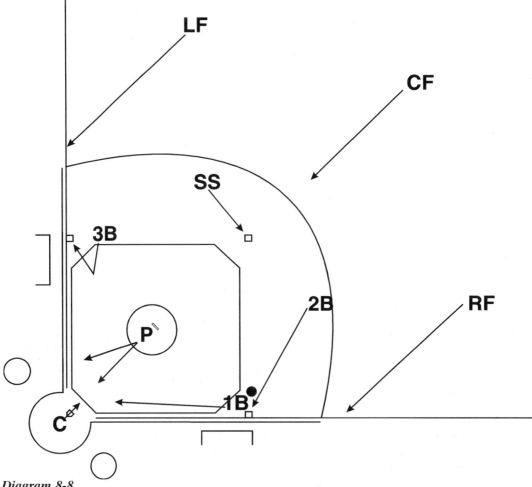

Diagram 8-8

1) How hard the ball is bunted.

2) The pitcher's ability and range in fielding bunts. Some pitchers are better than others.

If the third baseman reads the play and sees that the pitcher is going to field the ball, he must quickly break back to third and cover the bag like a first baseman. The pitcher now gets the lead runner. The left fielder should be in backup position in case of a wild throw (Diagram 8-8).

I know you want to know what happens if the third baseman reads the play incorrectly, breaks for the ball and ends up standing behind the pitcher fielding the ball. He must yell, "one, one, one" to alert the pitcher to throw to first base because we have to get an out.

The defense is trying to get the lead runner, but if the offense does its job, then the defense needs to counteract with an out. Remember, the team that allows the least amount of mistakes usually will come out on top. So build a sound defensive unit. If the other team doesn't score, you only have to produce one run to win.

Rundowns

When was the last time you went to the circus? If you have attended a baseball game and watched a rundown occur, then you probably have seen a first class circus. This play is probably executed improperly more than any other defensive maneuver. It seems very simple: catch the ball, run at the runner, throw to your teammate, make a tag.

For some untold reason the play seems to expand into several throws and catches until someone makes a mistake and the runner dashes quickly back into base ... safely. It reminds you of the movie *Smokey and the Bandit*.

The rundown play can be a very simple execution. The key is to try to make just one throw and no more than two.

There basically are two rules to remember:

1) Run the player back to the base he came from.

2) Try to make just one throw.

For example, if the runner was picked off first base, the first baseman would run at the runner and chase him toward second. Hopefully he would make one throw to the shortstop and get an out. I feel that this last method is the best way to execute the rundown play. If you can get the base runner to run at full speed, then it is impossible for him to put on the brakes and retreat in the opposite direction. Too many throws increase the chances for error which will allow the runner time to find a way out.

Photo 8-7

The first point to remember is to get both fielders on the same side. Notice in Photo 8-7 that the first baseman and shortstop are on the infield side of the base. This prevents the infielders from hitting the runner with the ball when making a throw to each other. For example, in Sequence 8-2, if the pickoff throw from the pitcher takes the first baseman to the outfield side of the base, then it is imperative for the shortstop to move to the outfield side, also. In Sequence 8-2 the shortstop is moving to the other side of the base.

After the first baseman has received the ball, he wants to start running at the runner, chasing him toward second. The key is to get the runner moving at full speed. This prevents that runner from stopping and changing direction quickly after the first baseman has made a throw to the shortstop. The first baseman must run with his arm up about his shoulder. From this position he simply tosses the ball to his teammate. If you run with your arm down by your side the throw will be late on a close play.

The reasoning is this: By the time you bring your arm up and throw the ball, you will be late more times than not. It also gives you a chance to control your toss and

Sequence 8-2

allows your teammate to see the ball at all times. I have seen a number of infielders run with their arm down and then all of a sudden here comes a throw from somewhere out of control. Keep the arm up and then give your teammate a toss with a stiff wrist which allows the infielder to control the toss. Try to toss the ball at your teammate's chest.

 ***Coaching point:*** *Never attempt a ball fake, because this only fakes out your teammate, not the runner.*

As the first baseman advances toward second base in pursuit of the runner, notice where the shortstop is positioned in Sequence 8-2. In Photo 8-8 he is one step in front of the bag. He doesn't want to leave his position until the ball is thrown to him. Then he will call for the ball by yelling "now" as he starts to move toward the oncoming throw. The key point here is for the shortstop to start to move toward the runner as he calls for the ball. The infielder moves toward the runner as he catches the ball. This keeps the runner from stopping quickly and advancing back toward first. If executed in this fashion it is impossible for the runner to get out of the rundown. The only possibility would be if one infielder dropped the ball.

Communication is extremely important on a baseball field if the defense wants to survive. The rundown play is no exception. Failure to communicate can be detrimental to the defensive club. The infielder receiving the ball must yell "now" when he wants the ball thrown to him. Remember, as he yells "now" he should have already taken a step toward the runner.

Problems occur when several throws are made. This is a breakdown in the technique which requires only one throw. From time to time it may take two or three throws. If this happens, then the infielder must follow his throw and get out of the way of the runner. The first baseman throws to the shortstop and gets out of the baseline and moves toward second. The shortstop now runs the base runner back toward first where the pitcher is covering. Remember, the pitcher must follow his first throw which was a pickoff throw that started the whole process. A smart base runner will try to find an infielder standing in the baseline without the ball to run into for an interference call. It is important to follow your throw and get out of the baseline so the runner doesn't run into you. If the play happens to take several throws, then the infielder would continue to follow his throws and rotate to the next base.

There are times when it is mandatory to make more than one throw. An example would be if the runner is picked off first or second base and immediately sprints for the next base. It is impossible for the infielder to start running toward the runner because the runner is more than halfway toward the next base. This happens a lot at first base with a left-handed pitcher. The base runner will break toward second on the first movement from the pitcher. If this happens, the first baseman must immediately catch the ball and throw it to the shortstop. Then the shortstop will run the runner back toward the first baseman covering. Hopefully the play will only take two throws.

The same principles apply between second and third, and third and home. The key is not to allow the runner to get in the middle and dance around. Get him going hard in one direction. If you can do that, then you will get more outs than not.

Remember, the pursuer should get the pursuee every time if the play is executed properly.

Passed Ball and Wild Pitch Defense

With runners on second and third how many times have you seen a pitcher uncork a wild pitch and stand there and watch the catcher try to retrieve the ball, throw wildly back to the pitcher allowing both runners to score.

At Tennessee we work countless hours on trying to either runner from scoring on a wild pitch or passed ball. In a close game this can mean the difference between a win or a loss. It is important for every infielder to know where he should go on a passed ball or wild pitch.

The field is essentially divided into thirds with the first baseman taking the right side of the mound, the pitcher covering the home plate area and the shortstop backing up on a wild throw which would take the other third of the infield. This play has been proven to be very effective in stopping the trail runner from scoring on a wild throw from the catcher to the pitcher. It is extremely important that the shortstop and the second baseman back up the pitcher.

On a wild pitch or passed ball, the defense automatically knows where they are suppose to be with runners on second and third. As soon as the ball gets by the catcher, the pitcher will break toward home plate while yelling either "1-1," "3-3" or "2-2," letting the catcher know where the baseball is. One would be the first base side, two would be right behind him and three would be the third base side. While he is running and yelling, he is also letting him know by pointing.

Once the first baseman reads the passed ball, he will break in and cover the right side of the diamond. The second baseman will break in and cover either second base or break in behind the mound looking for a possible wild throw from the catcher while the shortstop will break in and over toward second base behind the mound reading a possible wild throw. The third baseman will cover third base, the left fielder will come in and back up third base. The right fielder and center fielder will come in and back up the play behind second base in case of a possible throw back from the catcher.

Relays

The team that can play catch on defense usually is the team that minimizes mistakes and gives itself an opportunity to win the ballgame. It is imperative for the position players to keep the ball off the ground. I have said many times that one good throw leads to another, just as one bad throw leads to another bad throw. It is ironic, but many times you will see an outfielder one-hop the relay man and the relay man make a bad throw to the catcher; whereas a good crisp throw from the outfielder to the relay man usually results in a perfect strike from the relay man to get the runner out by two steps.

Relays and cutoffs require a lot of practice and teamwork to be executed properly. I have found that many times an outfielder misses a cutoff man giving the offense an extra base which leads to the go-ahead run which in turn usually wins the ballgame. It is crucial for the outfielders to try to keep the double play in order and keep runners out of scoring position by hitting the relay and cutoff men.

The relay man is usually the shortstop or second baseman going out into the outfield on a double-cut situation. This is when a ball has been hit into the gaps or over an outfielder's head requiring the shortstop and second baseman to go out into a tandem and become the relay men.

On balls hit from right-center field to the right field line, the shortstop is normally the trail man and the second baseman is the lead on the relay tandem. On balls hit from left-center to the left field line, the shortstop is the lead man and the second baseman is the backup approximately 30 feet behind the shortstop. As the shortstop and second baseman break out into the outfield, the lead man on the tandem must glance back quickly to see where the play is originating. Is there going to be a play at third base or at home? He wants to take quick glances as he runs and sprints toward his position ready to retrieve an extra-base hit from the outfield.

Sequence 8-3

The trail man (second baseman) can also be the eyes of the lead man (short-stop). As he sprints out, he can help line up and give some verbal information on where he thinks the play will originate. He will be the last person to see where the ball needs to go because the lead man will be focusing on the trajectory of the throw from the outfielder. (Sequence 8-3)

The lead man on the relay needs to have his arms up, ready to receive the throw, yelling, "Let me have it! Let me have it!" so that when the outfielder comes up with

Photo 8-8

the baseball he sees the shortstop or second baseman as he prepares to throw the ball to the relay man. (Photo 8-8) The shortest distance between two points is a straight line, so it is imperative that the tandem (shortstop, second baseman, relay team) get into a position that puts them in a straight line between an outfielder and the base that the ball is going to.

Also, the relay man should already be turned toward his target with his hands out ready to receive the ball and make a quick throw by shuffling his feet and throwing to the appropriate base. This clearly gives him an opportunity to be quicker. Instead of catching the ball, having to rotate sideways, shuffle his feet and then throw, he is able to cheat a little which speeds up and makes the difference in a bang-bang play. I think it is important that the relay man take quick shuffle steps as opposed to a crow-hop which allows him to be quick as he throws the ball to the appropriate base.

Notice in Sequence 8-4 the middle infielder turns sideways as he sees the trajectory of the throw and gets into position to receive the ball and quickly shuffles his feet and follows the throw. Also the back relay man goes to a knee (Sequence 8-3) to allow a better view and does not block or hinder the throw or the relay man.

Sequence 8-4

> **Coaching Point:** *I feel like the key to having a successful relay from the outfield to the middle infielder to get the runner when he is going from third to home plate is to keep the ball off the ground. Make quick, crisp, accurate throws and make sure you are in a position to start the tandem as quickly as possible.*

Cutoffs

A relay occurs when a middle infielder takes a throw from an outfielder and relays the ball to another base in an effort to put out the base runner. A cutoff occurs when an infielder, usually the first or third baseman, stations himself between the outfielder and the plate to cut off the throw.

The purpose of the cutoff is to prevent the hitter from advancing an extra base on a throw to the plate. If you didn't have a cutoff man, the runner or hitter could advance into second base just about every time.

Photo 8-9

The cutoff man should assume a position approximately 50 feet from the catcher in a direct line from the throw from the outfielder. He must get there as quickly as possible with his hands up ready to receive a throw. The cutoff man should anticipate the play and realize that he must be ready for any type of throw: short-hop, ball left or right, and be ready to move his feet and be ready to move into position and catch the ball on his glove side ready to turn and throw to the plate. Or, as in Photo 8-9 he might have to catch, turn to his right side and throw a ball back to second or first base trying to get the next runner or hitter rounding first or second.

The communication from catcher to cutoff man is extremely important. If he wants the ball to come to the plate the communication will be as follows: If the catcher says nothing, the cutoff man knows that the ball is to go to the plate untouched. This is the reason why we want the outfielder to be about 50 feet from home plate. If the ball hits him in the chest with a good accurate throw it should get to the catcher on one hop and keep the hitter from advancing to second. If he wants the ball to be cut and thrown to the plate, he yells "relay" which tells the cutoff man to cut the ball and throw to the plate. If he wants the ball cut and thrown to another base such as first, second or third, the catcher will simply yell "cut 1," "cut 2" or "cut 3." This lets the cutoff know that he should cut the ball and throw to the appropriate base.

The key here is for the outfielders, middle infielders and cutoff men to play catch. Keep the hitter off second base and out of scoring position where it only takes one base hit to get him home. If he is at first base it takes an extra-base hit or a couple of singles to advance the runner home.

So the key to effectively executing the cutoff and relay system is to keep the ball off the ground and hit the cutoff man as quickly as possible.

Pop Fly Communications

It's not unusual to see the ball popped up in the infield or outfield and neither has an idea as to who has priority or who should make the catch. It is very simple if you put in a verbal system and spend time letting your infielders and outfielders know who has priority over certain areas.

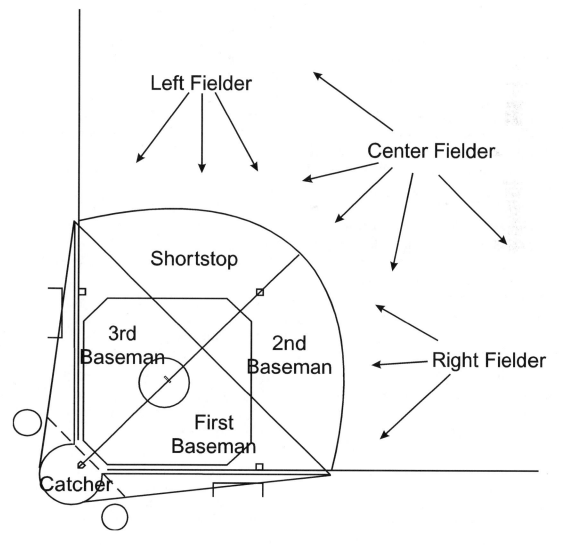

Diagram 8-9

Basically, the priorities are as follows:

- The first baseman has priority over the pitcher and the catcher.
- The third baseman has priority over the pitcher and the catcher.
- The shortstop has priority over the third baseman and the second baseman.
- The second baseman has priority over the first baseman.
- The center fielder has priority over the left fielder and the right fielder.
- All three outfielders have priority over the infielders when charging in on a ball hit behind the infield.

Diagram 8-9 shows where the infielders and outfielders have priority.

Key points to consider when the ball goes up is to wait until the ball reaches its highest point before calling for it. If you have time, an infielder or outfielder should yell three times so that everybody around knows who is going to catch the ball. Many times an outfielder or infielder converging on the ball only call it once. If they call it simultaneously, neither one hears the other. Calling it three times will allow the one infielder or outfielder to call the other one off the ball.

A general rule for pop-ups between the outfield and the infield is that if the outfielder calls for the ball, he takes it. We do not like for our infielders to run into the outfield for the ball. The rule here at Tennessee is that you go for the ball until you hear something. If the outfielder wants the ball, he will call you off. If you do not hear him call for the ball, then it is your ball and go get it.

It is much easier for an outfielder to catch a ball coming into the infield than for an infielder to catch a ball going into the outfield. Also, the outfielder is in a position to throw back into the infield where there might be a player tagging up to advance to the next base. If the outfielder calls for the ball it is his ball, although we do not want him to come in and call off a middle infielder who is already positioned ready to make the play.

The ball that we really want the outfielder to come and get is the ball that the infielder is still running for and is drifting out into the outfield. That ball must be caught by the outfielder. He must be aggressive, come and get it, try to call off the middle infielder and make that catch.

This takes a lot of practice. One of the things we do at Tennessee is put the Atec rookie machine at home plate, put our defense out in the field, throw pop-ups and let them work on game-like situations. They work on balls behind the first and second basemen. In some situations, the second baseman calls the first baseman off, in others the outfielders will call the infielders off.

It is critical that your team is in a game-like situation and has to communicate with each other to execute a pop-up defense properly. Five to 10 minutes two to three times per week will provide enough opportunities to prepare your team to make the proper communication on a pop-up in the infield or outfield.

First and Third Defense

The first and third defense is one of the toughest plays to execute. The offense will either start the runner at first or start both runners to create confusion on the defense, and wind up either putting the runner at first in scoring position or executing a double steal.

There are several points for the defense to consider in this situation.

- Which of the runners, the one at first or the one at third, is the fastest?
- What is the score?
- Is the runner at third the tying or the winning run?
- What are our weaknesses on defense?
- Does the catcher have a strong arm?
- Do the middle infielders have the ability to cut the ball off and throw to the plate?

All this must be taken into consideration before putting on a defensive play, and it must be done before any pitch is made.

Under normal conditions, if the runner at first has good speed, the offense will try to steal second base and hold the runner at third. But if the runner at third has good speed, the offense may use a delayed motion by the runner at first or put the runner in motion to try to draw a throw to second base or to a middle infielder and have the runner at third break for the plate.

Before we put on a play, our catcher verbally tells our defense which runner has the speed. He lets them know the possibilities with good speed at third or good speed at first. This alerts the defense as to what strategy the offense might be contemplating.

The three things we do at Tennessee are:

1) Throw through to second base.

2) Throw back to the pitcher.

3) Arm fake and throw to third.

As I have said earlier, several factors dictate what might be happening with the play. If the runner at third is the tying or winning run, we will never throw through. We are going to go right back to the pitcher or arm fake and throw to third.

Another important factor is whether it is early (first or second inning) or late (seventh inning and beyond) in the game.

If a runner breaks early when the pitcher becomes set and the runner at third is the tying or winning run, we are in a red zone. We going to arm fake at second hoping to entice the runner to break from third. As we turn back we hope to have him in a rundown with an opportunity to catch him for the third out of the inning.

It is important for our middle infielders to come in on a first and third situation if we are throwing through to second base. They must be able to read the runner breaking for the plate and come up and cut the ball and throw to the plate. The third

109

baseman can help by yelling "Home!" or "4-4-4!" if he sees the runner breaking. This will let the middle infielders know they must cut the ball and throw to the plate.

When this happens, the middle infielders will cut the ball off by catching it in front of the bag, setting their feet and throwing to the plate. If the catcher is throwing back to the pitcher, he must come up, set his feet and throw a chest-high strike that is hard enough to make the runner at third think the throw is going to second. (Sequence 8-5)

Sequence 8-5

If the catcher is arm faking and going back to third base, he must come out and arm fake the throw to second then readjust his feet and throw back to third in an effort to catch the runner sleeping or in a position where he is too far away from the bag.

This is a defensive play that needs to be practiced often.

Situations: Relays and Cutoffs

Situation 1

Single to left field, nobody on base

Pitcher .... Moves halfway between the mound and second base.

Catcher .... Reads the play and move toward first base to back up a possible throw from the middle infielder to a possible throw back to first.

First Baseman .... Makes sure the runner tags the base and then looks for a possible overthrow from the left fielder into second base. Also, he must be aware of a possible quick throw back from the middle infielder to get the runner at first on aggressive turn.

Shortstop .... Covers second base and take a throw from the left fielder.

Second Baseman ... Will back up the center fielder's throw to the shortstop.

Third Baseman ..... Protects third base area and look for a possible deflected ball from second base.

Center Fielder ...... Backs up left fielder.

Right Fielder .... Backs up the throw from left field while moving in behind second.

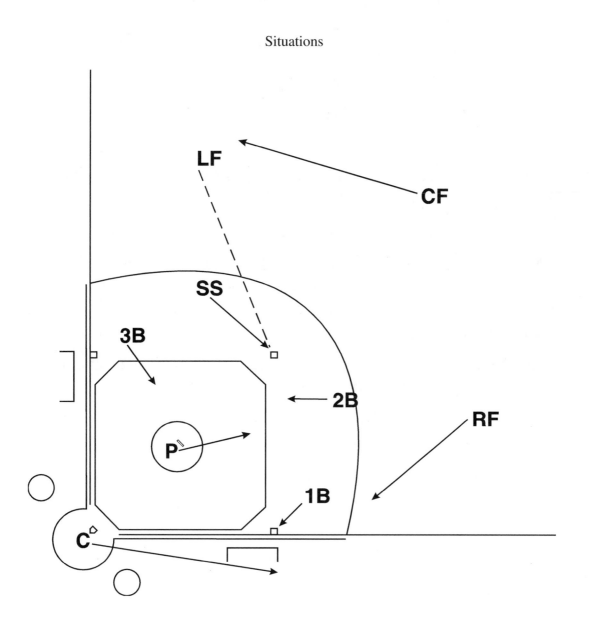

Situation 2

Single to left field, man on first base

Pitcher .... Backs up third base.

Catcher .... Remains at home plate and protects the area.

First Baseman .... Covers first base.

Second Baseman ... Covers second base.

Shortstop .... Moves into a cutoff position and lines up to throw to third base.

Third Baseman ..... Covers third base.

Center Fielder ...... Backs up left fielder in case a ball gets by the left fielder.

Right Fielder .... Moves in behind the second base area anticipating a wild throw on an attempted pickoff.

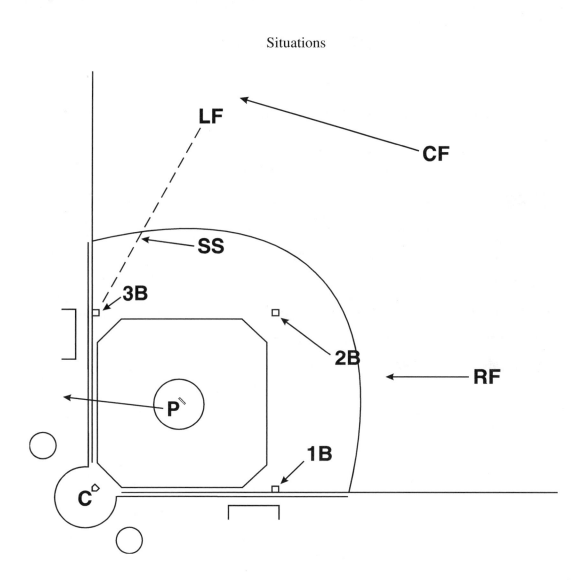

Situation 3

Man on second, first and second, or bases loaded — single to left field

Pitcher .... Backs up home plate.

Catcher .... Covers home plate.

First Baseman .... Covers first base.

Second Baseman ... Covers second base.

Shortstop .... Covers third base.

Third Baseman ..... Moves into cutoff position and becomes the cutoff man.

Center Fielder ...... Backs up left fielder.

Right Fielder .... Moves in behind the second base area looking for possible throw back to second

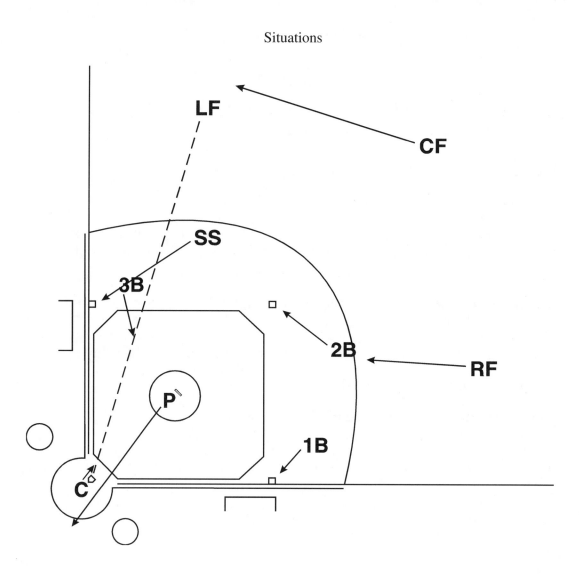

Situation 4

Double, possible triple to left-center, nobody on base, or man on third or second, or second and third

Pitcher .... Backs up third base line.

Catcher .... Protects home plate.

First Baseman .... Trails the runner to second base and covers the bag. Is ready for a throw back from one of the middle infielders on a runner taking too big of a turn.

Second Baseman ... Trails shortstop approximately 30 feet behind and lines up to throw to third base.

Shortstop .... Goes out into left center and becomes the relay man.

Third Baseman ..... Covers third base.

Center Fielder ...... Converge on the baseball.
& Left Fielder

Right Fielder .... Moves into an area behind second base looking for a possible overthrow.

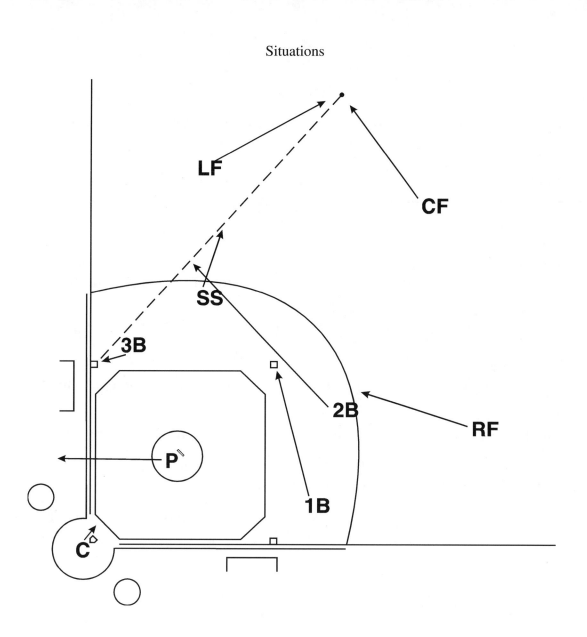

Situation 5

Double, possible triple to left-center field, man on first or second or bases loaded

Pitcher .... Goes halfway between home and third base and read the play.

Catcher .... Protects home plate.

First Baseman .... Trails the runner to second base and covers the bag on a possible throw from an in fielder on a big turn at second base from the runner.

Second Baseman ... Trails the shortstop approximately 30 feet and helps line up the throw to home plate or third base.

Third Baseman ..... Acts as the eyes of the second baseman and helps him to know where to throw the baseball.

Shortstop .... Goes out into left-center and becomes the lead relay man.

Third Baseman ..... Covers third base and stands on the outfield side of third base ready to receive a throw.

Center Fielder ...... Converge on the baseball and communicate on who takes
& Left Fielder   the ball.

Right Fielder .... Moves into an area behind second base.

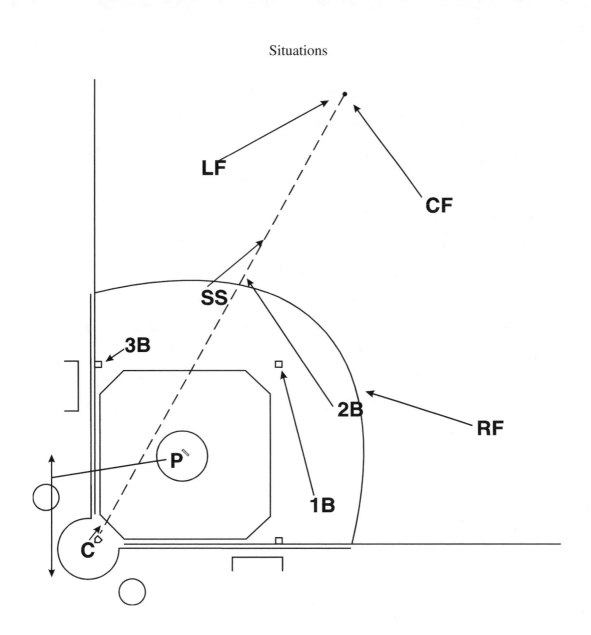

Situation 6

Double, possible triple down left field line, man on first

Pitcher .... Backs up home plate.

Catcher .... Covers home plate.

First Baseman .... Trails runner and covers second base.

Second Baseman ... Is the trailer behind the shortstop.

Shortstop .... Is the lead relay man.

Third Baseman ..... Covers third base.

Center Fielder ...... Moves in behind second base area in case of possible rundown or overthrow.

Right Fielder .... Backs up and moves in behind second base looking for a possible overthrow.

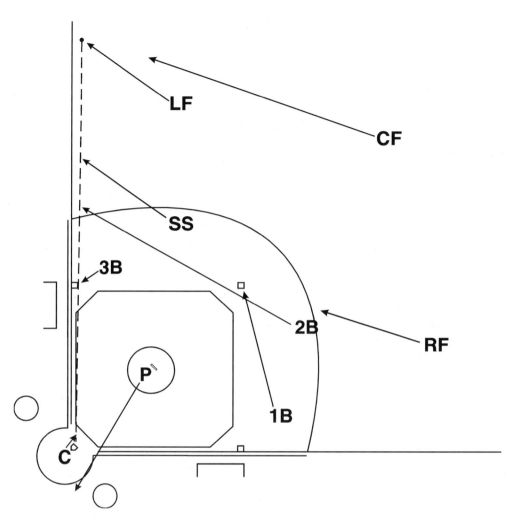

Situation 7

Single to center field, no one on base

Pitcher .... Moves halfway between mound and second base.

Catcher .... Protects home plate.

First Baseman .... Moves into the infield side of the base making sure that the runner tags first and then looks for a possible relay throw from a middle infielder on a wide turn.

Second Baseman ... Backs up the center fielder's throws to the shortstop.

Shortstop .... Covers second base and takes throw from a center fielder.

Third Baseman ..... Remains in the third base area.

Left Fielder .... Break toward center on possible backup.
& Right Fielder

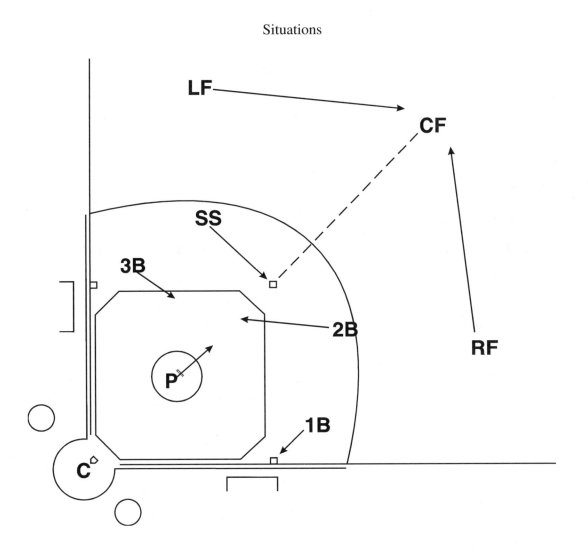

Situation 8

Single to center field, man on first base

Pitcher .... Backs up third base.

Catcher .... Remains at home plate.

First Baseman .... Covers first base.

Second Baseman ... Covers second.

Shortstop .... Cutoff man on a throw from center field to third base.

Third Baseman ..... Covers third base.

Left Fielder .... Break toward center on possible backup.
& Right Fielder

Situations

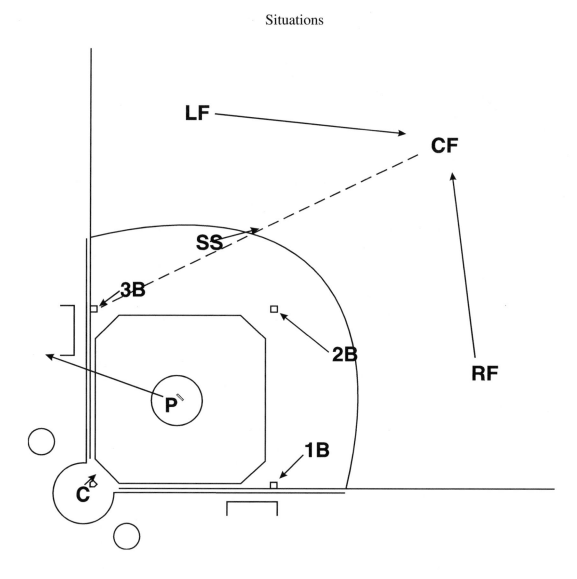

127

Situation 9

Single to center field, man on second, or men on second and third

Pitcher .... Backs up home plate.

Catcher .... Covers home plate.

First Baseman .... Is the cutoff man on the infield side of the mound to keep the ball from hitting the pitching rubber.

Second Baseman ... Covers first base.

Shortstop .... Covers second base.

Third Baseman ..... Covers third base.

Left Fielder .... Back up center fielder.
& Right Fielder

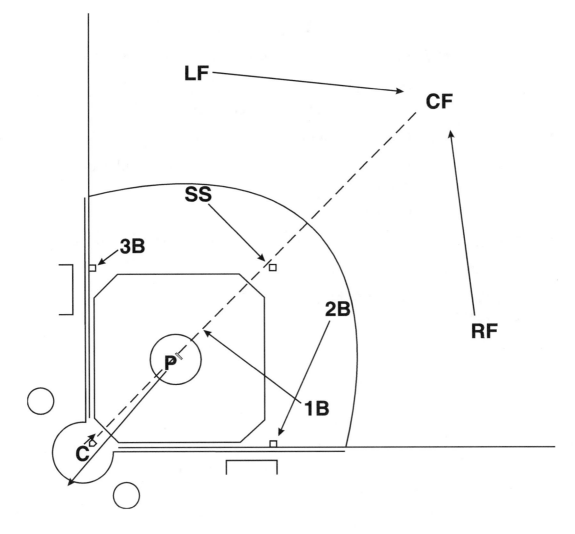

Situation 10

Single to center field, men on first and second or bases loaded

Pitcher .... Goes halfway between home and third and then reads the play and backs up that base.

Catcher .... Covers home plate.

First Baseman .... Moves in behind the pitcher's mound and becomes the cutoff man.

Second Baseman ... Covers second base.

Shortstop .... Will be the cutoff man on a possible throw to third base.

Third Baseman ..... Covers third.

Left Fielder .... Back up center fielder.
& Right Fielder

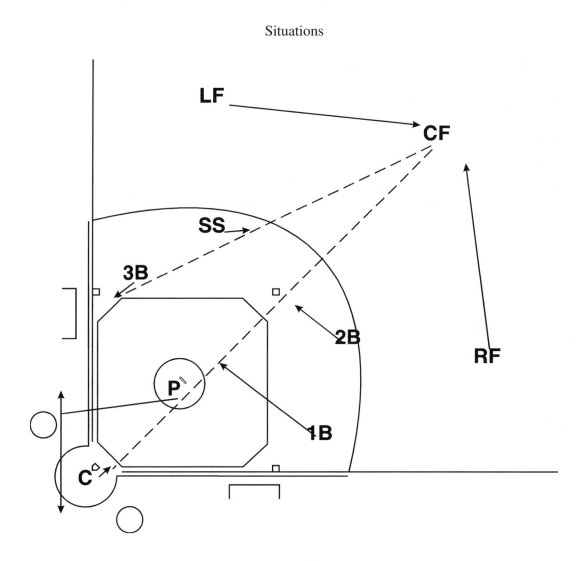

Situation 11

Fly ball to center or right field

Pitcher .... Backs up home plate.

Catcher .... Covers home plate.

First Baseman .... Is the cutoff man.

Second Baseman ... Covers first base.

Shortstop .... Covers second.

Third Baseman ..... Covers third.

Left Fielder .... Back up center fielder.
& Right Fielder

Center Fielder ...... Backs up right fielder on a fly ball to right.

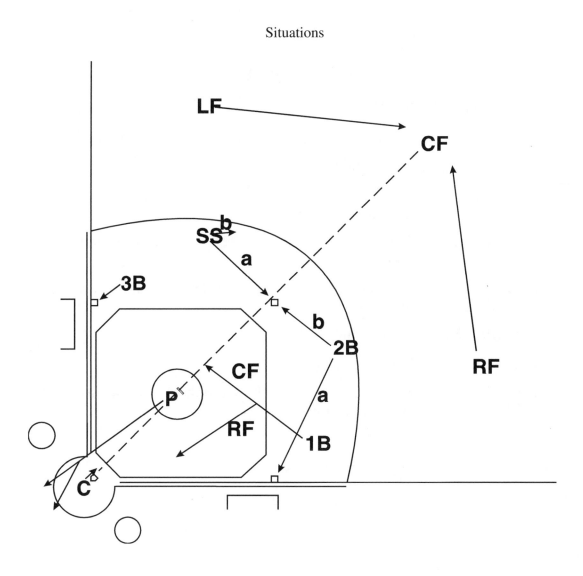

Situation 12

Single to right field, nobody on base

Pitcher .... Moves in on the shortstop side of second base.

Catcher .... Covers home plate.

First Baseman .... Makes sure the runner tags the base and then moves in and covers first base.

Second Baseman ... Covers second base and receives the throw from the right fielder.

Shortstop .... Backs up the right fielder's throw to the second baseman.

Third Baseman ..... Covers third base.

Center Fielder ...... Backs up the right fielder.

Left Fielder .... Moves in behind the shortstop/third base area to receive any wild throw.

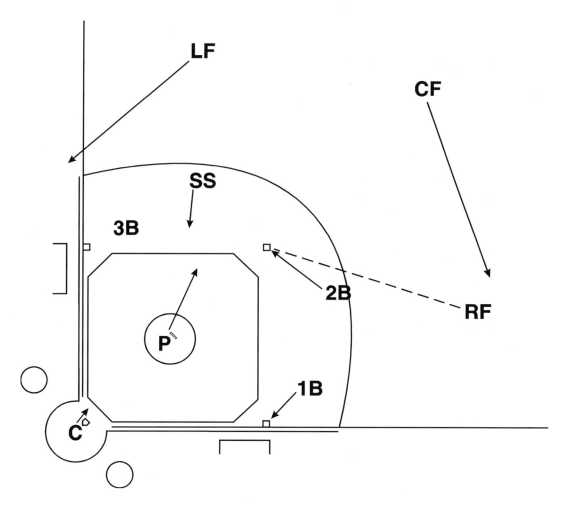

Situation 13

Single to right field, man on first or men on first and third

Pitcher .... Backs up third base.

Catcher .... Covers home plate.

First Baseman .... Covers first base.

Second Baseman ... Covers second base and also makes sure the runner tags second base.

Shortstop .... Moves into a cutoff position and a straight line between the right fielder and third base.

Third Baseman ..... Covers third.

Left Fielder .... Moves in behind third base as a back up.

Center Fielder ...... Backs up the right fielder.

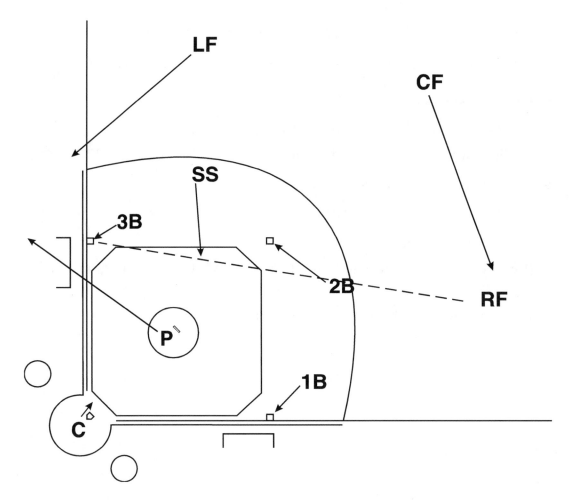

Situation 14

Single to right field, man on second or men on second and third

Pitcher .... Backs up home plate.

Catcher .... Covers home plate.

First Baseman .... Takes cutoff position between first base and home.

Second Baseman ... Covers first base.

Shortstop .... Covers second.

Third Baseman ..... Covers third.

Left Fielder .... Moves in behind second and third base area and reads play.

Center Fielder ...... Backs up the right fielder.

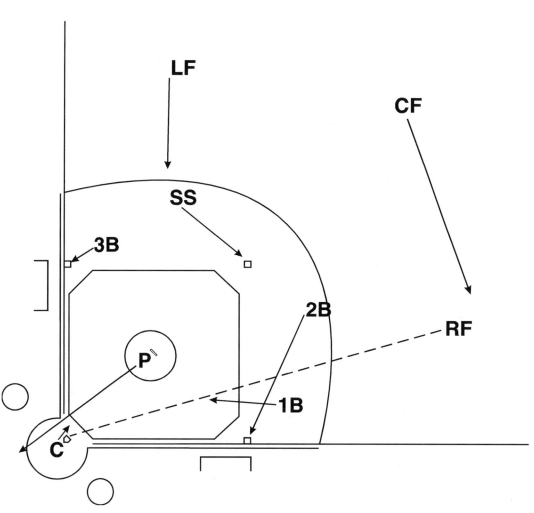

Situation 15

Single to right field, men on first and second or bases loaded

Pitcher .... Goes halfway between third and home and reads the play, then backs up that appropriate base.

Catcher .... Covers home.

First Baseman .... In cutoff position to home plate.

Second Baseman ... Covers second.

Shortstop .... Cutoff man to third base.

Third Baseman ..... Covers third.

Left Fielder .... Backs up third base.

Center Fielder ...... Backs up the right fielder.

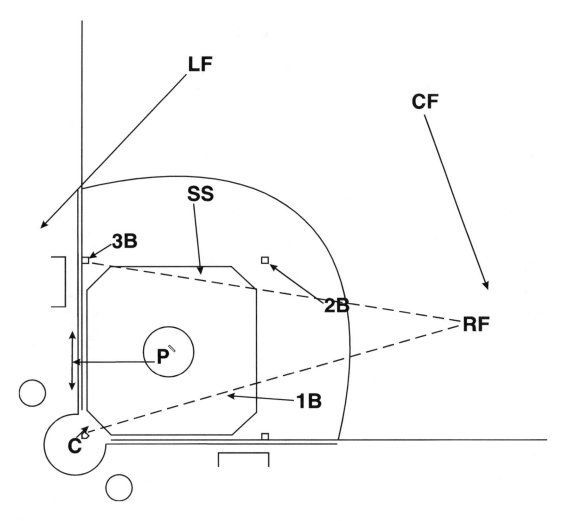

Situation 16

Double, possible triple to right-center, nobody on base, or man on third, or man on second, or men on second and third

Pitcher .... Backs up third base.

Catcher .... Covers home plate.

First Baseman .... Trails a runner to second and covers the base ready for a back cut from a middle infielder.

Second Baseman ... Goes out into right-center and is the lead cutoff man.

Shortstop .... Trails the second baseman approximately 30 feet behind and helps line up throw.

Third Baseman ..... Covers third.

Left Fielder .... Moves to third base area as a backup.

Right Fielder .... Backs up the center fielder.

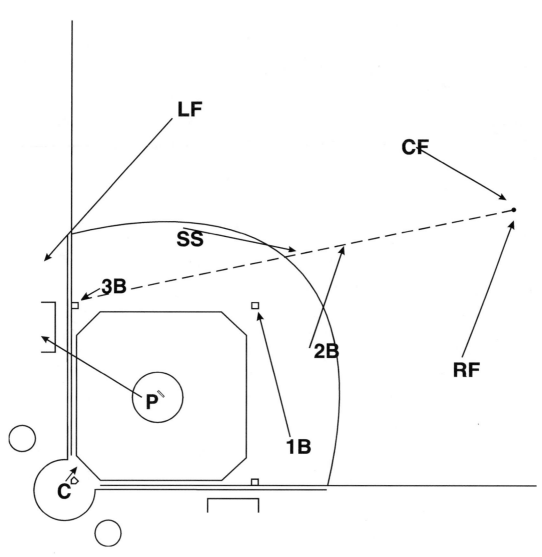

Situation 17

Double or triple to right-center field, man on first, men on first and second, or bases loaded

Pitcher .... Goes halfway between third and home to see where the throw is going; reads play and then backs up the appropriate base.

Catcher .... Covers home plate.

First Baseman .... Trails runner to second and then covers the base.

Second Baseman ... Is the lead relay man.

Shortstop .... Is the trail man behind the second baseman, approximately 30 feet.

Third Baseman ..... Covers third.

Left Fielder .... Moves into the area behind third base as backup.

Right Fielder .... Converge on baseball.
& Center Fielder

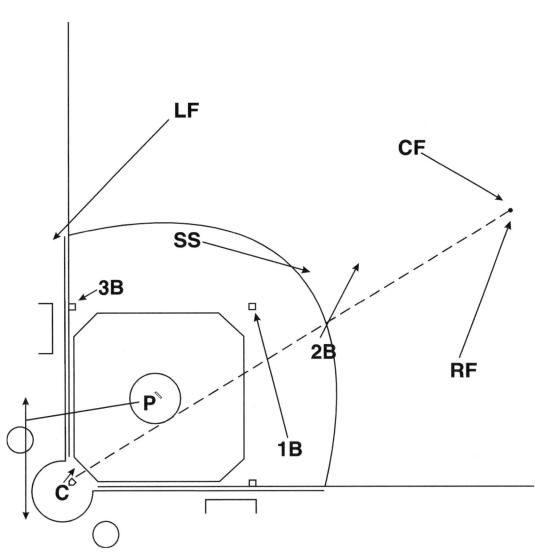